HOW CAN I FIND A LITERARY AGENT?
AND 101 OTHER QUESTIONS
ASKED BY WRITERS

ANSWERED BY
CHIP MACGREGOR

with
Holly Lörincz

The Benchmark
Press

CHIP MACGREGOR is a leader in the publishing industry, ranked on *Publisher's Marketplace* as one of the top selling literary agents in the U.S. He owns MacGregor Literary, one of the most successful agencies in the country, but he started his career almost thirty years ago. He has written over ninety published titles, worked as an agent with Alive Communications, and was a publisher with Time Warner Book Group. His current list of clients reads like a *Who's Who* of bestselling and award winning authors, and he is popular as a keynote speaker and workshop instructor at national writing conferences.

HOLLY LORINCZ is a literary agent with MacGregor Literary, and the owner of Lorincz Literary Services, an editing and publishing company that regularly works with NY Times Bestselling authors. She is also an award winning novelist, a nationally recognized speaking coach, and a long-time writing instructor.

HOW CAN I FIND A LITERARY AGENT
And 101 Other Questions Asked By Writers
by
Chip MacGregor and Holly Lörincz

2015 © The Benchmark Press

For more information about this book or the authors, visit
http://www.chipmacgregor.com

ISBN-10: 0996119205
ISBN-13: 978-0-9961192-0-7

MacGregor Literary Inc.
PO Box 1316
Manzanita, OR 97130

Cover Design by
Keri Knudson, Alchemy Book Covers

Interior Design by
Holly Lorincz, Lorincz Literary Services

DEDICATED
to Steve Halliday, who got me into the book business;
Carolyn McCready, who gave me a job;
and Rick Christian and Greg Johnson,
who taught me how to do it well.
Nanos gigantium humeris insidentes.
—Chip

to Chip MacGregor,
who told me he liked my voice.
—Holly

TABLE OF CONTENTS

TABLE OF CONTENTS

INTRODUCTION

You're at the airport, settled in for a five-hour wait, red lining the latest draft of your Great American Novel. The man next to you, some guy with a fedora, pulls out his own manuscript and red pen. You make eye contact. Oh. It's *that* guy. The guy with the blog. The guy Publisher's Marketplace regularly lists as one of the top literary agents in the United States. Chip MacGregor of MacGregor Literary.

You will likely never have this chance again. You turn to him and smile. "Hey, do you mind if I ask you some questions?"

The landscape in the publishing industry has shifted and blurred in the past decade. Writers, from novices to seasoned veterans, are struggling to redefine their job, their goals, and their role in the process. Agents can help. One agent in particular, Chip MacGregor, has been involved in publishing for thirty years—as a published author, a longtime editor, a publisher with Time Warner Books, and the current owner of a successful literary agency. He is well known for staying in front of the changing paradigms and freely offering support to writers, hosting a high-profile industry blog, and speaking on the writing conference circuit. He's researched and answered thousands of writing and publishing questions collected from blogs, conferences, interviews, emails, phone calls, and, yes, airports. If *you* were lucky enough to sit down with him over coffee, what would you ask?

The following is a collection of the top one hundred and one questions literary agents are asked every year . . . and some that should be asked.

A note from Chip:

I'm a literary agent, so I'm considered either an "experienced" or a "biased" cog in the publishing machine, depending on your position. I've made my living as an author and, later, as an editor and publisher, before I fell away from the Lord and became a literary agent (a vocation often lumped in with lawyers and car salesmen). I was with one of the top literary agencies in the business for many years, and now I'm out on my own. I admittedly have my own perspective.

I'm fairly successful at what I do, in a business where some people call themselves "agents" but seem to be working from a limited knowledge base and, consequently, don't last very long; I'm well known in the publishing world and, over the years, MacGregor Literary has developed a solid reputation. Yet, most people who know me will tell you I'm not an agent evangelist. I happen to know there *are* some very good things a literary agent can do for you, but I'll be the first to admit not everybody needs an agent, though this decision should come from an informed position, not simply because you want to skip the middle man. So, Holly Lorincz (a fellow agent and professional editor) and I have gone through the thousands of questions and notes I've collected over the years—questions being asked to agents by all manner and level of writers—and culled out the most important and timely issues every author should consider in today's market.

Be prepared, you're about to get my opinion.

PART 1

WRITING FOR PUBLICATION

"Seriously, what does the publisher really want?

A great idea, expressed through great writing, by an author with a great platform. And, of course, what they really want are books that make money, from authors who work hard and are easy to get along with during negotiations, editing, and marketing. There is no clearer answer: acquisition editors generally look for a manuscript in the genre they like, or try to find books with a certain style or voice that appeals to them, but every one of them want a great, salable idea by an author who can support it.

One breakout bestseller for a publisher can pull an entire line of small books along behind it—and if we could tell for sure which book was going to be that next breakout, like a golden glow emanating from the pages, our jobs would be a lot easier. Agents and editors *are* looking for fantastic writers, published or not, especially those with salable ideas who can produce regularly. But the thing all of us want most is a big book that will sell a lot of copies, so we can get those great books by newer authors onto the shelves.

"In a hundred words or less, what is the best writing advice you've received?"

For me, that's easy. On page seventy-one of Strunk & White's *Elements of Style* (Third Edition), they give this advice: "Write with nouns and verbs, not adjectives and adverbs." In the words of E.B. White, it is nouns and verbs that "give to good writing its toughness and color." In his insightful work *On Writing*, novelist Stephen King goes into great detail on this advice, pointing out that any reader can understand a combination of a noun and a verb: "Mary sighs." "Computers crashed." "Books illuminate." In my experience, authors (particularly novelists, but ALL authors) tend to use adjectives and adverbs to dress things up when they can't find the right word. But that's nothing more than lipstick on a pig. The right word is what good writing is about. I'm not saying denude your text entirely, just be judicious. If you want punch and strength in your writing, write with nouns and verbs.

"You work with a lot of successful authors; have they shared any good writing tips?"

Vince Zandri, who has done numerous bestselling novels and sold more than a quarter million books, wrote to me and said, "The best writing advice I ever got came from Ernest Hemingway in the form of his memoir, *A Moveable Feast*. If writers are worried about one thing, it's the ability to keep a story moving from day to day. To avoid the 'block,' as some people call it. Papa wrote slowly and methodically in the early morning hours, and trained himself to stop at a point where he knew what was going to happen next. That way he could be sure of getting started the next day—and it left him the afternoons to play, exercise, fish, drink, or do whatever he wanted."

Successful nonfiction writer Mel Lawrenz wrote to say, "The best advice? Take the long view. See the long process of publishing as an advantage—the stages of writing, editing, rewriting, and revising make for a more refined end product. Don't miss the opportunity to rethink what you originally wrote."

Harlequin author Dana Mentink sent this: "The best writing advice I got as a pre-pubbed author was that I should act like a professional. My mentor encouraged me to treat my writing like a business, not a hobby. Put in the hours, describe yourself to others as a writer, and really put yourself into the mindset of a professional. She explained to me that there's a big difference between 'I want to write a book' and 'I want to be an author.' The latter requires professional dedication."

Children's author Kayleen Reusser noted, "Believe in yourself, even if no one else does. At my beginning, I was the only one who believed I could write and get published. Even my mother told me I could not write—no money, no time, three small children to care for. But I swore I would die trying. (Thank goodness it has not come to that.)"

And novelist Dianne Price wrote to say, "Know your characters. Live with them. Talk to them. Listen to their words and the cadence of their speech. Make them your constant companions. Argue with them. Commiserate with them. Ask them questions. You must know them to make them believable."

"What do you recommend for a writer who wants to improve his or her craft?"

Write more. I find most writers write a bit, but the best writers tend to have written a *lot*. Read more. I find most every writer reads some, but the best writers tend to have read a lot, and have read *widely* and not just in their genre. Also, shut up and listen to advice, don't immediately reject a reader or editor's suggestions/thoughts. Then practice mimicking a successful author's style, or shadowing the structure and storytelling found in a famous novel, just to see what it's like to be someone else. Great art tends to be derivative. Study great writers to see what you can glean from them.

"What inner qualities do you see in your most successful authors?"

What a fabulous question. Um . . . a longing for truth. A willingness to work hard. A desire to improve. An attitude that listens and doesn't get whiny every time somebody suggests an editorial change. A desire to explore the big questions. A boldness to be brave and try something new. Those are the qualities I probably see in most successful authors.

"What makes a topic universally popular?"

In the world of publishing, we have what we call "evergreens." Evergreens are the topics of interest that remain popular with readers year after year, decade after decade. Nonfiction books on money, health, relationships, purpose, living more effectively, and finding spiritual peace always seem to resonate with people. And every generation needs its own voices, so every few years the culture needs new books on those topics. In addition, what works for one may not work for another, so alternative viewpoints create publishing opportunities for more writers (that's why one person can write a book that tells you she lost weight eating nothing but meat, and another can write a book claiming she lost weight cutting meat from her diet).

I think you need to write to a universally felt need. That means you might write a book that says, "I want to save money," or "I want to lose weight," or "I want to feel closer to God." Think about the needs and desires common in our world. "I want to feel better and have more energy," and "I want to worry less," and "I want to find something interesting to do with my life," and "I want to experience healthier relationships." Think of the needs we all share, the emotions we feel, and you'll be on your way to locating an evergreen topic.

When I worked as an editor at a big publishing house, you could assume every season one of our imprints would do a personal finance book. We were going to have a handful of diet and exercise books each year. We were going to offer a book aimed at helping people develop better relationships, another for those looking to organize their life, and something else aimed at the shifting roles of a mother. Why cover the same ground each year? Because people want something new, that speaks to their current situation. And yes, I'll grant you it's funny, since there is a similarity in the answers. Every diet book basically offers similar information: eat less, move more. Every finance book presents the same basic solutions: spend less, save more. Every organizational book gives similar guidelines: clean out your closet and buy a calendar. Sometimes an author will come up with a whole new way to approach an issue. Other times you're simply repackaging answers for a new audience. But you're always going back to those frequently asked questions.

Someone recently wrote to ask if evergreens work with magazines—and they definitely do. Take a look at any popular woman's magazine: You'll find health stories ("ten tips to trimming your thighs" and "how to lose that belly forever"), money stories ("how to invest in an IRA" and "cheap places to take your family on vacation"), relationship stories ("discover what he really wants" and "how to talk heart to heart"), faith stories (how some celebrity found peace), and multitudes of self-improvement stories (checklists, to-do's, ideas to try). You'll also find reviews, sexual insight tough to put into a book, and stories on travel. All evergreens, all useful when moving into magazine writing.

One thing to keep in mind is that every magazine has a unique readership, so almost every article you write will have to be reshaped in some way. It's rare you write one article and sell it to ten different magazines with the same wording . . . but every professional knows you can use the same basic article and create ten or fifteen similar stories in order to fit the magazine specs or reach the correct audience. My friend Dennis Hensley, who runs the Professional Writing Program at Taylor University in Upland, Indiana, has sold his time-management principles more than a dozen times—to teachers, to realtors, to car salesmen, to builders, etc.—and each time the article was adjusted to contain a unique slant for that magazine's readership.

"If there are no new ideas for writers, how do we come up with original stories?"

Who said there are no new ideas? For that matter, who says we need new ideas? Every romance is about two people meeting, getting pulled apart by something, then discovering they must be together because . . . geez, because we ALL want to have a magical romantic story like that. As I said, every health book is about eating less and moving more. Every finance book is about spending less and saving more . . . and those books continue to sell. I think chasing after the latest idea is a trap. You're better off becoming a great writer, and writing the best story you have in you, in my view.

"Can you tell us what books are selling right now? What are the trends you're seeing?"

I can try. I purposefully go to the Book Expo of America (BEA) and Romance Writers of America conference (RWA) yearly so I can try to keep up on the new trends. In the ebook space, it's pretty clear contemporary romance, romantic suspense, and suspense thrillers of all types are selling well. That would include PI novels, police procedurals, crime novels, etc. So, what we call "category" fiction (that is, fiction that follows certain rules for its genre) really leads the way in ebooks. It's nice to see literary fiction is finally starting to sell well digitally. For a long time, there was a sense people weren't buying literary novels on their Nooks and Kindles, but we seem to be beyond that now.

Of course, the whole notion of fiction on ereaders is not just a trend, it's an established fact in the contemporary world of publishing. We thought fiction was outselling nonfiction about 3-to-1 on ereaders, and that was the figure I often used at conferences. But a study was made recently that showed fiction is outselling nonfiction roughly *8-to-1 in the ebook market*. Wow. My guess is that people who are used to reading things electronically are simply getting a lot of their nonfiction information (recipes, health tips, medical advice, etc.) on the web, leaving them to seek fiction for their ereaders.

In the print space, we're still seeing the fiction bestseller lists ruled by familiar names. Nearly every big book these days is from an author who has had big books in the past, which seems frustrating to a lot of novelists, but that's just the nature of the business. When a book breaks out (and there are always going to be breakout novels—see *Gone Girl, Hunger Games, Fifty Shades of Grey,* etc.), we add a new name to the list. But aside from the breakout novels, we're still seeing romance, suspense, and thrillers selling well. Of course, literary fiction tends to dominate the print bestseller lists.

Other trends would include much more colorful and artistic covers. A focus on "relationships" and "body image" dominating nonfiction titles. A renewed interest in history, including both the big events in history as well as the overlooked, interesting bits. Niche publishers popping up to give readers what they want via ebooks (such as noir novels or westerns). Intriguing TV stars doing books. A strong interest in religious titles in general, especially books about heaven and "proof" of the afterlife.

One interesting exercise is to try to track the top twenty novels on the bestseller list in order to discover what fiction readers want. It's pretty clear the general market likes tension-filled stories and insightful growth/coming-of-age tales.

Meanwhile, those on the CBA side seem to like emotional romance stories (Karen Kingsbury, Beverly Lewis, Lynn Austin, Tracie Peterson) and exciting-but-not-racy suspense novels (Irene Hannon, Dani Pettrey, Joel Rosenberg).

Now, having said that, keep in mind I don't think authors ought to chase a trend—by the time your book is written, that trend will probably be on the way out. Instead, focus on the story you've been given, even if it first seems like your story may not be trending at the moment. And, of course, my best advice is to stay away from advice from people like me, since that is the one thing that's SURE to screw you up.

"Can a person who does not aspire to fame be a successful writer?" Of course. Some writers are looking for fame, but in my experience most get into writing because they have a story to tell. By the same token, some writers embrace the fame aspect of getting published, and love the attention it creates, while others hate it, and just want to write and maintain their privacy.

There are plenty of examples of both. Perhaps this is getting skewed today because of social media, which can sometimes make it seem like every author is required to be an extrovert. But my feeling is there are a lot of introverted writers who don't seek to be everywhere, all the time, commenting on everything.

"How do you set up your writing business? What are the benefits to treating your writing business as a 'real job' by setting it up in a professional manner? And what did you do to make that happen?"

Let me offer a handful of thoughts based on personal experience . . .

- You're doing the right thing by asking questions. Finding some folks who have done this before is a good way to start. Begin by talking to people who have already been down the path. Ask them what they've learned.

- Find a place to write. Make this your official writing spot and designate it as your official home office, then read up on what the IRS will allow you as a tax deduction.

- Establish a writing time. For most authors, that's simply "morning." Protect a time each day when you can do some actual writing and not just check email, do phone calls, meet people for coffee, etc. When I started, I set aside 6:00 to 8:00 every morning. (I had young kids. Later that would not have worked. I hate mornings.) Tom Wolfe starts writing at 9:00 and stops at noon. Find a time that works for you, in which you'll just WRITE, and not make phone calls, do emails, or Facebook.

- Create a filing system. Alphabetizing your research notes and direct quote by title or author works well. Some nonfiction writers create files based on sub-topics, or simply on chapters. Don't rely on the "Eureka!" system.

- Set up a bank account just for your writing business. Sign up for PayPal. Perform all business transactions via these two accounts, providing a clean record of activity when it comes time to do your taxes.

- Set up your address list. Keep emails and phone numbers handy. And, if you want to move into the bold new world, invest in a phone that will keep those handy.

- Create a calendar. Not just for your day, but for the big projects you've got. It'll help you figure out what you're writing when.

It'll also remind you that you've got to take Fiona to her orthodontist appointment, and what night the Snyders are having their party. For me, the biggest benefit is that by scheduling deadlines into my calendar, I feel accountable to those deadlines.

- Group similar activities. Do all your mail at one time. Group your phone calls back-to-back so you get through them quickly. Ditto email, if that's possible. Any task that you consider "occasional but regular" should be scheduled—for example, I try to look at submissions every Friday morning.

- Create a budget. How much do you expect to make this year? How much do you expect to spend? (Having more of the former makes for a better business, by the way. I know, crazy stuff.)

- Create a to-do list. Every day. Work through it. On Friday (or every other Friday) start at the bottom and work up—that'll prevent you from never doing the one task you hate.

- Create a contact list. Capture names and email addresses, so you can stay in touch with the people in the industry who matter. Then add those into the aforementioned address list.

- Invest in a separate business phone line or business cell phone. It becomes annoying to your family when you constantly answer your personal phone with "MacGregor Literary. This is Chip."

- Invest in a website and business cards. I don't know if you really need a blog, but you certainly need a site where people can find out about you and connect with you.

- Invest in the help you need—training or people or space or tools. For instance, how well do you know your writing software? Have you figured out how to create sections to control your page numbers yet? No? Consider taking a workshop on how to use Word.

- Invest in a great computer and the software you'll need. If you work in publishing, you'll need Word. Hence the training.

- Invest is a good printer, preferably with a scanner.

- Invest in yourself—take a class, attend a conference, join a support group, get therapy, whatever it is you need to grow.
- Learn to keep good records. If you need a class on it, take one. There are even personal organization trainers who will help you get organized
- Learn about the specific taxes for your situation so you track income and expenses, and learn to maximize information. If you're making money as a self-employed writer, you're going to need to be paying quarterly taxes, so ask a bookkeeper or accountant for some help.
- And the BEST advice? Write regularly. If you don't do that, you won't make a living at this.

"I was told at a conference that every fiction genre has 'rules.' Is that true? And how would I know what the rules are?"

The entire concept of genre fiction holds that each genre has certain rules to which most novels must adhere, as there are concepts and scenes every reader has come to expect when they pick up a western, or an action adventure, or a romantic thriller. The different rules distinguish the genres. So the rules for a traditional romance would include that the hero and heroine must meet early in the book, and that they must get together at the end. The rules for a cozy mystery include something bad (usually a murder) happening at the start of the story, an amateur sleuth will have some suspicions and start to look into it, and the mystery will be solved at the end of the story.

So, yes, every genre has rules. You can find the rules by doing a search on the internet using the terms "tropes," "convention," "rules," and your main genre area—for example, Urban Fantasy conventions are listed on a number of blogs and websites; Harlequin maintains a list of rules for romance writers on their website, and they are very specific.

Most new genre writers are safest when sticking very close to these rules, until their publishing record is firmly in place . . . but even then they're taking a risk that loyal readers will not appreciate any toying with their expectations.

"How do you define literary fiction?"

Generally speaking, literary fiction encompasses novels that do not have rules. Also, these are novels that explore the great questions of life—who am I? why am I here? does my life have meaning? what should I be doing? who is God? why does He allow such pain in the world? Most literary fiction will offer characters we care about, exploring the great questions of life, and making choices, then examine the ramifications of those choices on the lives of the characters.

It's a way for me, as a reader, to explore my own life in a deeper way by seeing things through the lives of other people. That's what great literature does—causes us to think more deeply about life, see things in a new light, and offers some sort of insight into the great questions.

"What determines if a book is YA or adult?"

Normally there are two issues involved: themes and characters. Young Adult novels have young characters, and the story tends to focus on certain themes—coming of age, the transition to adulthood, exploring sexuality, fostering independence, self-identification, problems at school or with parents, or society's authorities, etc.

YA themes are almost always black and white, with a clear good and a clear evil, or a defined problem with a clean-cut solution. Adult novels are more nuanced, complicated, and (hopefully) worldly, while focusing on more adult themes, like love in a grey, sometimes confusing world. For instance, no one thinks *The Road* by Cormac McCarthy is YA, though one of the main characters is a child.

Again, good novels have themes directly relatable to the intended readership. YA novels have younger characters, as traditionally the protagonist is the age of the target reader, though some YA fantasy has late-teens characters suddenly dealing with independence or self-identity issues. Evaluate your novel in light of theme and characters, and you can usually figure out where it should land.

"What makes a novel move from the midlist graveyard to the bestseller list?"

Great question! Of course, most early novelists would be perfectly happy to be in that midlist graveyard, as you call it. There are plenty of writers who make a good living in that midlist. But while most folks would probably answer you with statements like "a great story" or "incredible ability," I don't know if I can point to many common denominators that automatically move a novelist to the bestseller lists.

I've seen dynamite stories go nowhere, and I've seen really crummy writing sell extremely well. Clearly, this isn't an exact science. But since I don't want to answer with something like "a great marketing effort and a committed sales staff," I'll encourage you to do one thing: improve your craft. I know, I tend to say that a lot. An author doesn't always have control over some of the things that will happen to his or her book (store placement, which chains pick it up, who chooses to review it, etc.), but the one thing an author *does* control is the quality of the manuscript. I'm convinced greatness will break out—a great writer *will* get discovered. That's been proven time after time. So, if you're feeling a bit stuck, consider what you could do to improve your writing. It's still the best investment an author can make.

"What is the definition of a book series? Does it have to be an ongoing plot involving the same family or character, or can it be a series of similar stories in the same era? Can I take a book that's become too long and divide it into three, thus creating a series?"

First, there is the CONTINUING STORY. That is a series of books following one story arc. Tolkien's *Lord of the Rings* is an example of that type of series, as is *Hunger Games* and *Divergent*. In this type of series, either the story is too big to contain in one book, or there are a bunch of story elements that continue and need to be completed in order to wrap up the series—the Harry Potter books are a good example. While each book tells its own story, there are bigger story lines that continue throughout.

Second, there is the CONTINUING CHARACTER series. That's a series of books sharing characters over a number of books. There are numerous examples in detective fiction, where Hercule Poirot or Travis McGee or Sherlock Holmes or Kay Scarpetta solve a new crime in each book. There are also examples in children's literature, where Winnie the Pooh or Curious George or the Boxcar Children or Artemis Fowl experience a series of adventures.

Third, there is the COMMON STORY series. That's when similar stories (a bunch of mail-order bride novels, for example) or settings (a number of old west tales) or theme (several books about immigrant experiences, or great romantic meetings) tie together a number of books. To be fair, this can sometimes be nothing more than a publisher's marketing department deciding to link several novels together that happen to all be set in mid-century Texas—but it's still a "series," as far as the market goes. The advent of ebooks has made series more or less a necessity. Readers with Kindles and Nooks prefer series fiction, so we're now seeing every publisher push for good book ideas to be turned into series.

"Can you tell me your process when you write a nonfiction book? I need help creating a system in order to help me finish my book."
Okay. I like to sound smart, so I find a plethora of people smarter than me, and pay attention to what they have to teach me on the subject. Then I decide if I have something new or unique to add to the conversation, and if it's important enough for a book.

Keep in mind that, when writing nonfiction, I generally know the basic direction I'm going. Otherwise, why should I be the one writing the book? I get my notes and junk out, look at the pile, and get depressed because I'm certain I'm never going to be able to turn that heap of crud into an actual book anyone would ever buy, so why not go drink a Guinness and watch another rerun of *Law & Order?*

Days later, I'll look at it again, feel guilty, and start organizing it into piles. Creative ideas. Boring idea. Insightful ideas. Ideas that are linked together. At this stage, I find myself creating new categories, collapsing categories, finding supporting research, tossing some of the inappropriate or off-topic notes. I'm familiarizing myself with my material.

The next step is to give it scope and sequence, so I generally rinse my mouth with Scope and wear sequins. (Ha! Is this guy a laugh riot or *what?*) I put down on paper some sort of general outline, which gives me a framework. That outline will change roughly thirty-seven times before the book is done, but I've always found it easier *to change something already written* than to create something new. It's been shown that the table of contents is the single most important factor in helping a reader make a decision to buy your nonfiction book, so I make sure the TOC makes sense in terms of "what will I cover" and "what order will I present it."

Once I have the outline, I "explode" it—that is, I start putting notes and quotes and stories and points in each section. I move the junk from random piles into piles connected to the stream of information in the book. This goes on and on until I don't have anything left to say (which can sometimes take as much as seven or eight minutes). I try to take time with this part, adding additional notes (even more stuff than I can use), assessing where the book is strong and where it's obviously weak. I continue exploding my outline until I realize it's all there, in one form or another. The stack of papers and notes I'm looking at are, in essence, my book. It's an extended outline, with my material in order. Then I just have to sit down and turn the outline into a book. So I start to write. More or less.

For the record, I know several nonfiction writers who simply take their outline and talk through it, then turning the recordings over to somebody else to convert the words to the page. I could never do that, since I find "talking" and "writing" to be separate skills (which is why I can't seem to use those helpful software programs that promise to save my hands from further injury). It works for some nonfiction writers, so if the actual wordsmithing is getting in the way, try this approach. Just remember, we buy books, not speeches. The two things are as different as playing golf on a field and playing golf on a video game.

Either way, at this point you are simply working through the material you've already put into place. You'll find that elements will shift as you go along—one point feels out of place, another feels inadequate. That's fine. At this stage, you're just trying to get everything down onto paper. Don't think about rewriting at this point, just squeeze your brain dry.

This is important. Once I start writing, I go *all the way through the book*. I don't stop to edit or revise. The point is to get the bulk of the words down on paper, usually leaving me with a crappy draft. My goal at this stage isn't to produce an award-winning manuscript—it's to get a crappy draft *done*.

I can then take my oh-so-stinky draft and make it better. But, if I stop along the way to do major revisions, I find I never actually get done. So a crappy draft is better than an unwritten-but-potentially-brilliant manuscript. Once I've worked my way through the first draft, I set it aside for a few days, sober up, and let myself come back with a new perspective. Then I start editing, sharpening, strengthening, and wondering why I ever said I'd do this stupid book in the first place.

Eventually, I have a bit-better-than-crappy manuscript, which I show to a trusted friend who has promised never to make fun of me. She points out why it's awful, yet never suggests a career in dry-cleaning might be a better choice. Then she gives it back to me with nice little notes to cheer me up ("this part doesn't suck as bad as most of it!"). Sooner or later, I take her notes to heart, and improve the lousy manuscript I banged out. And it gets better until (and God only knows why) the publisher agrees to take it.

Everyone establishes their own process, but feel free to borrow mine; it's worked for me. The Guinness part is really important.

"Do you have any suggestions on how to find and organize useful research from multiple sources? And what if one of those sources is a thousand-page biography I cannot remove from the library—will I have to make long-hand notes? And how do I organize the research after it's done?"

I can think of several suggestions I've learned from working on my own books, or from working with experienced writers on their projects:

- Useful information is collected in pieces. It often comes in short facts, like timelines, quotes, and interesting thoughts found in magazines, books, newspapers, interviews, etc. Therefore, I always take the approach that, in the beginning, my job is to collect scraps, with no thought to order or usefulness. That will be determined later, when you do what I suggested above and "explode your outline." But at the start, I'm just looking to collect all the info I can on my topic.

- If I see info as being a bunch of pieces, the best thing I can do is to write down and keep track of the pieces, thus the magic of 3x5 cards. Go ahead—call me old-fashioned; I still use a steno notebook when interviewing someone because it makes me look like a reporter in a made-for-TV movie. I do sometimes use my laptop to take notes, however, and I've learned to use Word and Excel and Evernote to help me control a bunch of facts in the computer version of 3x5 cards. But, in the end, I can't manipulate these scraps of text as easily as I can when writing stuff on small cards.

- On every card, I note my source. That way, I already know where it came from if I use the fact and need to footnote it.

16

- The cards help me to think holistically about my writing project. Rather than having a bunch of text on a screen and having to do a word search or scrolling around trying to find the one quote I need, I can spread out my cards and re-arrange them as necessary. Even if I have five hundred cards, I can take them and move them around, grouping them chronologically, topically, alphabetically, or simply in clumps of random piles that seem to make sense at the time. And I don't accidentally hit delete.

- Copyright law prohibits me from copying and selling someone else's information (particularly their unique expression). The gray area, and one generally accepted by researchers, is that copying documents for their facts and figures is probably acceptable, assuming you invested in the source. Or (and here it gets murkier), if you can't invest in the source because it's not available, that your copies are destroyed once you've decided how best to use the information in your own text. However, I know plenty of researchers who won't make hard copies because they fear copyright infringement. The Stanford University Libraries' website has an excellent page on library copying.

- I have sometimes used a camera to photograph a book spread—but be wary. The same copyright laws apply. I've never used a handheld scanner, but I have paid to have entire documents scanned, particularly when I need long quotations from source documents. Again, you must make only one copy of the document for the purpose of making notes or lifting cited block quotes, and then delete that document.

- I know this is a discussion of research and not copyright law, but a couple more things need to be said that relate. Kinko's paid millions of dollars in a copyright infringement suit because they were copying and selling the work of various writers. The point, as clarified by the judge, was that the professors who had requested the copying should have urged students to *buy the book*. In other words, it was unfair to authors to have somebody else making money on their work. They started asking people to sign a waiver whenever they asked Kinko's to copy pages from books. That caused a new suit, based on the fact that Kinko's was still profiting from illegal activity, even though they were making an attempt to push the legal issues onto the person requesting copies. The whole point is that you, the author, are the winner here. Instead of other people making money off your creative work, your rights are protected when the researcher is expected to buy your work. So when the government does things like shut down Napster for leeching the creative works of others, writers ought to applaud.

- And that leads to my last comment, a reply to the person who wrote to me and asked, "If I copy a page out of your book for research, would you be more concerned that I get your words right for my article OR that I copied a page from your book?" My answer: You know, I'd be concerned that you're not obeying the law if you don't ask my permission. I'd be concerned that, if you don't ask my permission, you're leeching off my hard work. I'd be concerned you're choosing to show no respect for the very laws designed to protect this profession. I've had too many of my words stolen, appearing in other people's books and articles and websites, to let this pass. I'm sick and tired of lazy writers failing to abide by copyright laws. That answer your question?

"When working on historical fiction, if an author is incorporating real historical figures, what is the author's responsibility to the character? I sometimes admit to feeling guilty of slander—my interpretation of their deeds and motivations is quite different than that of historians. What is the ethical line between historical fiction and history?"

Many authors have altered facts and dates in order to tell a better story—a novel isn't a textbook. There are no restrictions, no hard and fast rule stating, "you must have your facts correct" or "you must accept the commonly held notions about a historical figure's motivations." I do think, however, it is important for the author to know as much about the details surrounding the event and character as possible, so the changes he or she introduces are purposeful, rather than simply misstating a date or location out of ignorance. The informed author is then working within a pre-existing structure that can be remodeled, or possibly razed, but always with a nod to the original. That's what makes it historical fiction.

The author is inventing a story to entertain, maybe to explore themes and motivations, not to teach history. So, while I wouldn't create a story in which the Japanese attack Pearl Harbor on July 11th (unless it's a time paradox thing), I see nothing wrong with an author creating a story depicting an interesting twist—that Roosevelt knew about the attack ahead of time, or that the attack was led by a rogue group of Japanese military, or that it was all a mistake. With fiction, it's the story that counts. Besides, if we knew all the deeds and motivations behind historical events, there would be no need to explore them further. A novel allows us to consider alternative interpretations—that Richard III was actually a good guy, or that Sir Thomas More was a self-absorbed twit, or that Robert E. Lee wasn't the military genius he's been made out to be. Sometimes those ideas are daft (Oliver Stone's movie *JFK* was filled with tripe and innuendo that culminated in a weak, confusing storyline), other times the ideas can be reasonable (take a look at Josephine Tey's *The Daughter of Time*). But what your readers care about most is that the story is interesting, emotional, and readable.

I once had an author write a novel in which she made one of the giants of the medieval church out to be a bad guy—a letch and a schemer. The freelance editor objected, claiming we were somehow damaging the church by questioning the subject's character. But we argued (and the publisher supported) the notion that a novel is a complete work of fiction. So if we want to turn Abe Lincoln in a zombie killer, we can. If we want to make Richard the Lion-hearted a buffoon, what's to stop us? It's fiction. What matters is the story.

"Where can a writer find a competent, willing mentor? Most classes seem like they are geared toward novice writers. Conferences don't set you up with lasting relationships. Great writers are busy writing."

A mentor is somebody with whom you have a relationship. It's not as easy as wandering down to Mentors-R-Us and picking one up. Most of the mentors in my life have been people I came to know socially or professionally. We built some sort of relationship, and then I began to meet with the individual and learn from him or her. For example, I worked with Rick Christian (a well-known literary agent) for years. I got to observe him in various situations, ask him questions, clarify things, and see how he did his job. I didn't pattern everything in my life after Rick, but I learned incredibly valuable lessons regarding the role of an agent in the life of a writer. Some of the folks who mentored me spent considerable time with me, others spoke with me on the phone or shared wisdom via emails and letters. If you're expecting a mentor/protégé relationship to spring up after one meeting, you might have a few too many expectations of a mentor candidate.

Consider doing a few of these things . . . first, you might talk with the teacher of one of those classes you mentioned. The fact that he or she is in that sort of role might mean he or she has the ability and the interest level to begin a relationship with you. Second, consider joining a critique group, where other writers get together to review each other's work. Sometimes an experienced member of a group can give you some individual attention. Third, don't shun a conference. Those can be a great place to get face-to-face time with an experienced writer and begin talking books and words. And fourth, don't insist on a Pulitzer Prize nominee right off the bat. All you're really looking for is someone a bit further down the path than you are—someone with more experience or wisdom than you have, who can help you grow. Over time, you'll begin making new relationships, and find new mentors.

One last thought: You, in turn, need to invest yourself in someone else not yet at *your* level. I've found I grow the most professionally when I'm

20

forced to talk through the business, to mentally collect and organize that which you've already learned so you can share it. Every writer I know has had the benefit of those who have gone before. EVERY writer. I write the way I do because I was influenced by a handful of successful authors. I had a couple of dedicated teachers who committed themselves to helping me improve my craft. I had writers around me who shared from their experience. That's why I remind authors that all of us are creating things that are derivative—we're all building on the books we've read, the authors we've admired, the wisdom we've received. It's why I make it a point with the authors I represent to encourage them to share their own stories with other writers. I really believe we are helping build the next generation of authors.

"I've been lucky enough to find a mentor, a successfully published author. I don't want to waste her time, so what are some key questions or issues I should discuss with her?"

The easiest way for me to address this is to give you a list of the thirty things I came up with to help me stay focused when I'm talking with protégés. As a mentor, I know these are key issues new writers need to think about:

- The basics of sitting down to write (e.g., have a time, have a place, have a schedule, know what you're writing toward, etc.).
- The goal of writing (1000 salable words per day is a good start).
- Get it down on paper, revise later (don't rewrite your book while you're creating it).
- Give yourself short assignments (i.e., take a big writing project and break it into bite-sized chunks.
- The importance of crappy first drafts (remember, it is easier to revise than to create—so don't worry about the fact that your first draft is awful, just create that awful first draft and you're on your way).

- Story and plot. In other words, talking through the story to make sure writers understand a story arc, classic plot lines, and pacing.
- Creating great dialogue.
- Establishing your setting (I suppose this includes description and imagery in your writing).
- Creating strong characters.
- Instilling themes, morality, and depth into your fiction (having your characters explore the great questions of life and make decisions that are open to interpretation).
- Organization (how to organize your writing and your life).
- How to balance writing, ideas, and platform in your career.
- Original vs. adaptive creativity (the difference between coming up with your own unique idea and revisiting older ideas in a new way).
- The concept of "voice" (how you sound like yourself in print).
- Establishing relationships with other authors, editors, and collaborators (and possibly helping the protégé meet some of the folks in the industry).
- Getting to know the markets.
- How to get the most out of a writer's conference (and why it's a good idea to participate).
- How to create a great proposal.
- Why you should know publishers, the industry, and trends.
- Writing that sells.
- Selling your proposal.
- The role of literary agents (and I may possibly provide connections).
- Career planning for writers.
- What's in a publishing contract (how to read it, what it means).
- Negotiations (how to negotiate a contract, what a pre-negotiation is, how to prepare for it).
- How to market your book, with or without a publisher.

- Filling in the financial gaps (every writer has times when the money is lean—talk to writers about spending and saving, as well as explore ways to increase income through small writing projects).
- Everybody needs a more experienced person you can turn to with questions, a fellow writing friend, and someone to help who is not as far along as yourself. The famous American author Sherwood Anderson was mentored by Theodore Dreiser, while Anderson in turn mentored Ernest Hemingway and William Faulkner, and was a writing peer of Carl Sandburg and Gertrude Stein.
- A healthy perspective of a writing career (keeping in mind that publishing is not life).
- A system for working your plan, so you move forward in your writing and publishing.

In my view, if you cover these topics with writers, you'll hit most of the important stuff they need to know.

"Any advice on how to make a critique group faster and more productive? Are they worth it?"

Sure. First, let me explain what a critique group is: a collection of fellow writers who come together to improve each other's writing. (And, yeah, occasionally they come together to smack down the arrogant, or to make themselves feel better by criticizing someone else, but the goal of the group is to help everyone improve.) Sometimes you'll have only one or two people as your crit partners; other times, you might be part of a group that gathers on a weekly or monthly basis. You pass your work around ahead of time, the others make notes, then come together and share their assessment.

In my experience, nearly every writer benefits from having crit partners, whether they write fiction or nonfiction. And every writer needs to be prepared to show a work in progress, possibly even a piece that's just not working. Everybody has some bad work now and then. The point of the critique group is to improve. So get it out there—let your partners see your work. It will help them as much as it helps you, since they'll be able to see how you handle certain writing problems.

Years ago, in another life, I made my living doing dopey magic tricks and telling jokes. (Really.) I played some nice places (the Comedy & Magic Club of Hermosa Beach was one), and I played some awful places (insert the name of any smoky bar where the customers are more interested in Budweiser, Camels, and the opposite sex). One thing I noticed about the venues: even if the place was a dive, I learned lessons. Being in front of a living, breathing audience forces you to change your act. You have to work really hard to get people to laugh. All the rehearsal in the world wasn't going to cause me to perfect my act—for that, I had to go be bad in front of people, so I'd know to do it differently next time. Young performers come to understand this concept: *To get better, you need a place to be bad.*

There's a lesson there for writers. A lot of potential writers are simply too sensitive. As a writer, you need a place to be bad so you can learn to be good. If your ego is too fragile to allow someone else to read your work, it's time to learn this lesson. Allow yourself to be bad. Give somebody else (preferably not your mom, your spouse, or your best friend) the permission to be honest with you about your writing. Handing around a bad first draft is exactly the point of a crit group. Let them see what you're doing and offer some direction for your writing.

Yes, this takes courage. And it means you're going to have to find a couple people you trust. If you get into a large crit group, chances are you're going to have one person you don't like, who always hammers you for something. Learn to live with it. Paste a smile on your face, say "thanks very much," and move on to somebody whose opinion you actually care about. But somewhere, in the midst of all that fake niceness, be willing to at least hear what that individual has to say about your writing. A fresh set of eyes is exactly why you joined the group, so try to put your emotions aside and really listen to the criticisms, consider the merit of their points.

Scottish people have a saying: *learn to unpack a rebuke.* In other words, don't reject a criticism out of hand. You don't have to like it. You don't have to agree with it. But give it a little time. Take it and play with it. Be willing to at least examine the criticism and see if, just maybe, there's an ounce of truth in it. I found myself taking my own advice recently.

Somebody challenged me, saying, "You're playing it too safe on your blog! Where's the edgy Chip I've seen on other sites? You've pulled it all in, hoping this 'nice' Chip will be more appealing!" My first response? I slapped him. (No, not really. There I go again, playing it safe.) But my first reaction *was* to defend myself. "No, that's not true." Then I offered a bunch of reasons why I was still Mr. Edgy. Except . . . he was right. When I read back over my replies, I could see it. So I unpacked the rebuke. And now . . . um . . . I don't know. I'm not going to become Mr. Snotty, but I probably need to cut loose a bit more. I don't want people checking my site at bedtime in order to help them nod off.

Third, you asked how to make the critique group faster and more productive. As for "faster," send the writings out one week and talk about them the next week. Make it clear that each piece is allotted a certain amount of time for discussion, so it's fair for everyone. If you've got a Chatty Cathy, consider nominating someone timekeeper for each meeting. In terms of making things more productive, I encourage groups to write their comments. It's too easy to weasel out of a tough criticism when we're all sitting around the living room, drinking tea and commenting on Daphne's book, which may or may not be a prairie romance with aliens and talking dogs. Nobody wants to be the bad guy. Instead, ask people to *write their criticisms directly on the page*, then you can talk through them, and hand them to the author, before giving him (a) a Kleenex to wipe his eyes, and (b) the number of a good suicide prevention counselor.

Your result will be progress, not perfection. You ain't going to make it perfect. Seeking perfection in writing is what freezes people up and keeps them from writing (or from continued participation in an honest crit group). Aim for making it "better than last week."

Having a critique group can help you move forward. Besides, having writing friends gives you somebody to share your success and failure with. When those rejections come in, they'll pat you on the back and tell you that, yes, you're a fine writer, you just need to stick with it, and, hey, *The Art of Motorcycle Maintenance* was rejected by 105 publishers (which may or may not be true). Maybe they'll buy you a Guinness. (Another reason to like critique groups!)

"What is the difference between ghostwriting and collaborative writing?"

First of all, the term ghostwriting has really fallen out of favor. It became almost a derogatory term, suggesting the claimed "author" was a liar and too stupid to write his or her own book. This is not always fair or accurate for a person who chooses to get help to tell their story, especially when you consider just how difficult it actually is to craft an interesting, impactful message or story that will reach audiences—how many people who pooh-pooh ghostwritten books can actually write, quailing at the thought of writing a long memo to their company?

Think of it this way: A basketball player is famous because he can handle a ball and shoot, not because he can write. In that case, teaming him with someone whose skill set includes writing might be a pretty good idea. So the collaborator or ghostwriter was an accepted practice for a long time, especially when publishers wanted the focus to be on a celebrity, or that celebrity had too big of an ego to want to share the limelight.

There is definitely an argument to be made that excluding the writer's name from the cover is unfair to that writer, and also unethical as it creates a false perception to the people purchasing the book. Frankly, today, there is just no reason to hide the fact that two people collaborated on a project; it happens all the time, from light editing to heavy editing to hiring a collaborative writer to create a manuscript from notes and interviews. This does not negate the power of the author's story, it just means the author was smart enough to find a writing professional in order to create the best possible product.

"What are collaboration payment expectations?"

There's no "one right way" to get paid as a collaborator. I've done everything from a straight work-for-hire (the writer is paid a flat fee for creating the work) to the writer getting a split of the overall deal.

The amount paid will be based on several factors: how much work there is to be done, how much creative input the writer is expected to have, how long the book is supposed to be, how fast the manuscript is needed, etc. There are a huge range of alternatives, and I've worked on books where the writer was paid $5000 to step in and clean up someone else's work, as well as a book where the author was paid more than $100,000 to interview a celebrity and create the book completely out of thin air.

My experience is that most collaborative projects fall into one of three groups. The first is the "clean up" group, where a speaker has a seminar she wants turned into a book, or a pastor has a sermon series he wants turned into a book. There's already a bunch of material extant, and the writer is going to basically clean up what's there, clarify and fill in the gaps, and make it read like a book and not a series of speeches. These often pay in the $5000 to $15,000 range (though I'm sure people have done a heavy edit for less, or helped with the overall book concept and were paid more).

The second is the "create" group, when a writer interviews the author and writes the manuscript. These are the books you see on store shelves where it says the author's name with someone else. The author has the stories and content, but a collaborator was brought in to wordsmith the project. There are also opportunities for writers who are approached by publishing houses to create proprietary ideas, often with no author name on the cover. These types of projects most frequently pay in the $20,000 to $40,000 range.

The third group is the "celebrity" category—where a collaborative writer, usually skilled in memoir or journalism, comes in to work with a celebrity of some kind and tell his or her story. The pay can range from $50,000 to as much as $200,000, but these jobs are few and far between.

A collaborative writer can expect to receive a third of the money on signing, and the balance upon completion and approval of the manuscript (though sometimes a portion of the money is pushed out to publication of the book).

A lot of writers think they can be collaborators. Most cannot. You have to be able to tell a story in someone else's voice —a trick not everyone can master. You have to be able to see the big picture, and create a book that has a story line and clear principles, even though it's not your own. You have to be able to interview others, listen to them, and be willing to let someone else be the star. Above all, you have to be able to write fast and clean—collaborative writing is not for the slow creative who wants to mull over every artistic choice.

I used to make my living as a collab, and realized I was helped by the fact that I'd worked in magazines, where we had to interview people, think of interesting ways to tell the story, and churn out readable words under a firm deadline. In my experience, many of the best collaborative writers have some sort of background with magazine or newspaper feature writing.

By the way, if you're going to do some collaborative writing, you're going to need to know contracts, and you might find it particularly helpful to have an agent or an experienced publishing person assisting you in setting up the deal. Remember, if someone comes to you with a project to do for a speaker or a celebrity, they're going to view that speaker as the key person in the deal—you're just part of the book's production.

So, the speaker's interests, or the celebrity's interests, will come first. To make sure you get paid, get credit, and have your rights protected, you may want to talk the deal over with someone who has your own best interests at heart.

"I have a chance to collaborate on a book with someone who received a lot of media attention recently. But I don't know if his story is big enough to sustain a book."

Don't assume that because a situation has received media attention, the stories of the people involved will also be in the limelight. They might, but it doesn't always happen. I represented Lisa Beamer's *Let's Roll,* a book that hit #1 on the New York Times list, but the media focus on her was incredible in those days after 9/11. Lisa was on Larry King more than a dozen times in the year after the tragedy, so her "personal story" resonated with a public eager to learn more about her and her husband.

On the other hand, I helped Nancy Mankins tell her story, and my guess is you don't remember anything about her. Nancy's missionary husband was taken captive and eventually killed by Columbian terrorists. It's a well-told tale. The tragic event had received tremendous media attention, so it seemed a good risk at the time . . . but it languished in stores, as no one recognized the names of the people involved. Even a huge story like this, with a lot of media attention behind it, can fail to capture an audience.

So, my answer? It's hard to tell. But if you have to ask if the story is big enough, that might be answer enough.

"I have a chance to write a book with a celebrity. Does a project like that really help my writing career?"

If you come across a story that involves celebrity or heavy media attention, you might want to listen to the idea . . . but don't fall in love with celebrity. These are about the only personal story books with a chance of actually creating a payday for you, but it's not automatic. A buddy of mine was approached by a guy who owns a famous chain of fast food restaurants, and was invited to "tell the story" behind their success. He wrote the book, which was self-published and sent to all the franchise owners and managers (they sell a few in their restaurants). The book never made it into bookstores, never got media attention, and while the restaurants and personnel combined to make it a slightly profitable venture, the book didn't break out, didn't really move the writer's career forward, and didn't make him a lot of money. So be wary of saying "yes" just because someone is a celebrity.

And if we're talking about a former professional athlete, I can tell you first hand that (A) readers don't care one bit about an athlete the moment after he retires, and (B) nearly every professional athlete on the planet is hard to work with. I think it has something to do with being treated as royalty from the time they hit puberty—they don't live in the same world you and I do. They'll tell you it's because of living life in the fishbowl . . . from my perspective, it's because they make an obscene amount of money playing a game, and can never leave behind those heady days when they were heroes and everybody told them how wonderful they were. Be very wary of agreeing to do a book with a former athlete.

"I read that agents and publishers are more likely to accept submissions if an author has paid for an edit before submitting. I'm tempted to put my hard-earned dollars toward this idea, but I don't know if it would really help me get my foot in the door."

My response: You should do everything you can to make your submission the very best it can be, from proofreading to formatting to developmental reviews. Write and rewrite. Get advice from experienced authors. If you find critique groups helpful, join one and seek their input. If there is a good editor you trust, and you think you might learn something from his or her comments on your manuscript, by all means consider hiring that editor to help you with your work. My experience is that we all have myopia when it comes to our own work, and a good editor can often find the issues that we've overlooked or been unwilling to change. It's not necessary, of course, that every writer race out and hire an editor. But if you're stuck, it can be a great method for getting unstuck. And remember, professional editors are professional readers, proofreading while also scanning for what most casual readers won't notice when it comes to things like shaky plot points, genre conventions, or character arc. If you are sending off your manuscript to an acquisition editor, they have formatting and grammar expectations, and they use the state of a manuscript as a deciding factor. Typos and errors will likely lead to rejection.

For those of you that go the independent publishing route, the professional editor is a must. Nothing slows down sales more than a bunch of Amazon reviews bashing your grammar or typos or repetitive phrasing.

"Is it standard for most debut authors to have their manuscripts read by an outside copyeditor before the book goes to print? I've heard this is now common practice, but with the low advances publishers are now paying, it seems unfair to insist on the author funding the cost of an outside edit."

I think it's an exaggeration to say publishers "insist" on an outside copyedit. However, when a manuscript has been chosen for publication, the author is best protected when a manuscript comes in clean, so they're not relying on one over-worked, minimum wage, entry-level person to do the edit. And as the business has gotten harder, publishers seem to be doing less editing, and they love having their costs cut by having manuscripts come in as print-ready as possible. But I don't believe we can say that's any sort of official standard.

"How do I use a professional editor? How can I even find someone trustworthy?"

I'm going to turn this question over to Holly, who owns a successful editing business and is a published author. She is no stranger to the red pen. Holly . . .

This is a good question. Writers should know what to look for in an edit and an editor. First, decide if you need a developmental edit, a copy edit, or a proofreading (or a combination). For instance, it often makes the most sense to start with hiring a professional to do a developmental edit. Then, once you've taken their assessment notes and made plot or character or timeline revisions, you can decide if you still need to pay for a close reading (copy edit) or if you are ready to hire an editor for a simple proof (editing only for typos and grammar errors, not for content).

If you are looking for an editor on your own, make sure you talk to them before you sign up (you can find editorial services easily by doing an internet search). At least chat through email. What is their availability? What is their experience? How long does an edit with your word length generally take? How do they define the different types of edits (not everyone uses the same terminology)? How do they provide feedback? How do they charge? Are there testimonials available from previous clients? Do they edit from a hard copy (old-school) or can you send a Word doc? Do they need to see a sample first? Most importantly, do they work mostly with fiction or nonfiction? Will they be comfortable or open-minded regarding your content?

Once you have settled on an editor, and you're happy with the time frame of the review, be sure to communicate openly about what you think are problem areas. While a good editor will be reading the manuscript with basic novel or nonfiction concepts in mind, anyway, according to the type of review you've ordered, it's good to let him or her know you are particularly concerned with theme, or a minor character's voice, or a certain subplot, or scaffolding of information, etc.

Okay. You've just received your manuscript back, covered in red. What do you do with the professional edit?

To start, you may totally disagree with the suggested revisions but you still need to pay for the review. Remember, you are hiring for a service —a service that by its very nature is meant to tear apart your baby. When you've been handed back your bloody baby, you cradle it and cry and pound your chest in private, but then you sign the check. Now, if the edit is shoddy or unprofessional, by all means go back to the editor and do what you need to do. But if you take issue over their opinion, then you need to take a step back and reconsider.

Why did the editor say what he or she did? If this objective reader misread or found something needing repair, is it not then likely other readers will feel the same way? If so, consider the editor's suggestions or come up with your own revisions. Assuming your bottom line is to actually sell the book, will the general public agree with your editor or with you?

Once you receive the review, it is totally appropriate to email or call if you do not understand a comment or revision. However, it is not appropriate to make suggested changes and then go back to the editor and expect them to re-assess portions of your manuscript, not unless you've contracted them for their time. It's not that the editor is heartless or doesn't care about your project, but they do have other edits scheduled and need to move on.

A common response from authors is to want to explain their point of view or what they "meant" to the editor. This is totally not necessary. The editor's job is done the minute they tell you a scene or a phrase didn't make sense to them. The editor knows you will either see how it could be confusing and fix it or you will choose to ignore their suggestion. Either option is up to you—the editor has moved on.

When you find a good editor, learn to appreciate their work, even if it's emotionally hard to read his or her notes. The majority of us take our role as editor seriously, recognizing how vulnerable most writers are when it comes to having their work critiqued. That's as it should be. I offer criticism from the point of view of someone who honestly just wants to help authors produce their best work, never to be condescending or argumentative. I believe this is how most professional editors operate, from an innate desire to teach, to be supportive, and to be part of a book's journey to a bookshelf.

PART 2

THE ROLE OF THE WRITER

"What's the most important thing to know about publishing?"

I opened up my email recently to find a message that began: "If you could give me ten minutes of your undivided attention, the information you're about to view will CHANGE YOUR ENTIRE LIFE."

Well. I certainly could use my entire life changed. (For example, I'd like to be able to dunk a basketball.) But it turns out the author isn't going to make me taller or more athletic, nor is she going to help me glow in the dark or perform that great "floating lady" routine. She just wants me to look at her manuscript. And, unfortunately, it's not for a book. It's a play. And, um… we don't handle plays. And it's a "gospel play," though I don't know if that's really a genre. And the writer is not only looking for an agent, but for "investors." People wonder why agents and editors sometimes get cynical about projects in their mailbox? This is why. It's like the people who write to tell me about their poetry. I don't represent poetry. I don't even like most poetry. And there's no way for an agent to make a living selling poetry. Even if I love your poetry, I won't represent it.

So, while the details of my answer to this question might change from day to day, the basic answer remains the same: *Learn the industry.* Every few days I get a proposal that has been sent to a bunch of agents. We'll all be listed in the "to" line, sort of the publishing equivalent of asking for a date to the prom by posting an ad on Craigslist. A ten-minute search on the topic "how to prepare a query letter" would have helped this person understand that it's bad form to cc every literary agent in America. Read some trade magazines (Publisher's Marketplace, Writer's Digest, etc.), research the trends, understand the genres and who is representing or selling those genres. That's the place to start understanding publishing.

"What's the difference between a query, a pitch, and a proposal?"

I know, there's a lot of industry terminology kicked around and we sometimes forget new authors are also new to the lexicon.

A query: This is simply your attempt to get an agent or editor to look at your manuscript. You are querying them in hopes that they will pick you up as a client or that they will publish your book, eventually . . . but at first a query is nothing more than a request to have someone look at your material.

A pitch: When you query an agent or publisher, you need to pitch the book to them. The sales pitch is done in a brief email or face-to-face meeting (usually one or two pages, or two to three minutes), including the premise, a "need" statement, your qualifications, etc. (More on this under "I'm terrified of pitching.")

A proposal: If the agent or editor likes your pitch they may ask for a proposal, which you should have ready to give them. This is a document that contains information about the manuscript, market analysis, writing bio, synopsis, and some sample chapter. (You'll find more on this under "What are some key elements I should include in a proposal?")

"How do you find out who represents a particular author? And if I know an author who writes in my genre, is it okay to approach his or her agent?"

To find out who represents an author, you can go to AARonline.org (the website for the Association of Author Representatives) and look it up. Or you can go to Publishers Marketplace and check in the "deals" section. OR you can go to an author's website and see if he or she has the agent referenced somewhere.

But yes, agents tend to look for projects in the same genre—I represent several suspense writers, a bunch of inspirational novelists, and several literary novelists. I do a lot with nonfiction self-help, and some with memoir, sports, and crime books. Since I'm doing deals with editors at publishing houses who work in those genres, it only makes sense that I'd represent several authors who write in those genres.

"How can I prepare for conferences? I'd really like to woo an agent or editor into at least reading my manuscript."
Keep ten words in mind . . .

- READ. Don't just show up and wonder who the speakers are. Read the blog of the keynoter. Read the books of the teachers who are doing workshops. That way, when you hear them lecture, you'll already have a context for their information.
- RESEARCH. If you've signed up to meet with an agent or editor, check out their bio, see what they've acquired, and get a feel for the sort of books they like. By doing that, you'll be much more apt to talk with someone who is a fit for you and your work.
- ORGANIZE. Before you show up at the conference, look at the schedule and figure out what sessions you'll attend, which ones you'll miss (so you can share notes later), and when you can take a break to see friends.
- PRACTICE. When you sit down across from me in order to tell me about your book during a pitch appointment, it shouldn't be an off-the-cuff conversation. Practice what you want to say, how you want to describe your work, and what your hook is so you'll grab me.
- GOALS. Ask yourself what your goals are for this year's conferences. Don't just go with vague hopes. Plan to attend with some specific, measurable goals in mind. Write them down beforehand so you can evaluate yourself and your experience after you're back home.
- PROJECT. Come to the conference with a book you're writing firmly in your mind. That way, when you're listening to a speaker, you can apply the information to the project you're writing. Even if you later decide to write something else, the fact you've put the techniques into practice will help you improve.

- NOTES. Don't just sit in workshops and nod at the things you agree with. Take notes. Write down action items. Keep track of the ideas you like, along with thoughts for using them on your next project. If you make a note, you are six times more likely to follow up with the information you've heard.

- NETWORK. Every experienced conferee will tell you the opportunity to connect with other writers is one of the best aspects of a writing conference. So don't sit in your room by yourself—join in! Eat with others. Introduce yourself. Smile a lot. Chat up people in line. Tell people about your writing, then listen to what they are working on. Talk with others in the coffee shop or in the lobby. Publishing is a small industry, and the conference will have a bunch of people who work in it.

- LEARN. To learn is to change, so expect the conference to change you. Walk into every session expecting to learn something new. You don't know everything, so go expecting to gain new knowledge and skills. With that attitude, you won't walk out the hotel doors the same writer who walked in.

- INVEST. You're going to buy a bunch of books. (You may not think so, but you will.) So make that part of your budget now. They'll serve as a fresh motivator a few days after you're home from the conference and caught up on your sleep. ("Oh, look! A bunch of books written by my new friends! I loved hearing this author talk at the conference.")

One last thing to keep in mind at conferences . . . *be pleasant*. Don't be The Weirdo We're Talking About In The Back Room. There's frequently somebody like that at a conference—too friendly, too overbearing, too in-your-face. I remember one conference in Chicago where I had this guy right behind me all day long. Every time I turned around—bang! There he was, smiling. The conference staff finally had to pull him aside and ask him to tone it down before I felt the need to stab him with a pencil. Another time I had a guy follow me into the men's room, rambling on about his manuscript, actually sliding it in front of my face as I was standing at the urinal. Let me repeat: he slid it in front of me as *I was standing at the urinal.* (That's a true story, by the way. It's become sort of apocryphal in the industry, but it really did happen to me at Seattle Pacific University about fifteen years ago. I yelled at the guy, "NOT NOW!" I wish I'd turned to face him when I said it, if you, um, get my meaning.)

There's no sure thing. We all like pleasant people who we get along with and who show an ability with words. I think you stand your best chance to get noticed by an agent or editor if you spend time preparing to be that person.

"I'm terrified of pitching to an agent or editor face-to-face; I know I'm going to babble. Any tips?"

Holly is really the best person to answer this question. Not only does she listen to pitches at conferences regularly, she was recently pitching her own book, and she's a nationally recognized speaking instructor, with a number of awards under her belt. (Yes. I know. She's smarter than I am. Let's move on.) Pitching is really about your ability to speak on topic without passing out or making a fool of yourself. Umm . . . *my* best advice is to picture them in their underwear. It worked for Marsha Brady. Holly? Take it away.

All right, I'm going to piggyback on Chip's last answer about conferences. Before I was an agent, I was that sweaty, nervous writer hoping to win over an editor during a pitch appointment. I went in with my satchel stuffed with one-sheets, copies of the synopsis and the first fifty pages of my manuscript. I'd even made up clever business cards. I was dressed in a skirt and heels, trying to blend with the natives.

I practiced the heck out of my pitch, making sure I sounded comfortable and natural (though completely memorized) while describing the hook and unique premise in less than two minutes. I made sure the agents and editors I signed up to talk to were actually looking for books in my genre. Oh, I had done my research. I was prepared.

Shockingly, a good chunk of the writers were far less prepared. Or not prepared at all. They were showing up in cat sweaters, overalls, and unmatched socks. Worse, they didn't have writing samples. But worst of all, they didn't bother to prepare a short pitch, stumbling about like a drunks trying to recite the alphabet backwards. I'd watch the non-responsive agents out of the corner of my eye and wonder if the authors couldn't see the body language: crossed arms, leaning away, the rubbing of the temples, the yawns.

Now, I'm on the other side of the table, as a representative of MacGregor Literary, and I am still amazed at the number of writers who sign up to sell their book and yet come empty handed, *with no idea how to explain their project to me.* Don't get me wrong; I'm sensitive to the fact writers tend to be introverted, that a good chunk of us would rather be chewing on glass than trying to market ourselves. But don't shoot this opportunity in the foot. Get brave.

One way to help yourself while preparing a pitch is to assess your audience. What do they want to hear? What are their expectations? What might be their biases? For example, in this instance, you're addressing professionals—black-clad, suit-types who typically come from a big city. You don't *need* a suit (though I believe it shows respect and can't hurt) but you definitely need ironed dress clothes and brushed hair, an appearance that says, "I can meet deadlines and not come off as crazy on a talkshow." This doesn't mean cocktail dresses or tuxedos. It also doesn't mean overly sexy clothes.

I understand many people don't want to abandon their sense of self while dressing, but can you tone it down? Maybe wear a flamboyant scarf or pair of boots, maybe a flower in the hair . . . but leave the fruit-laden turban and train-wreck cleavage at home, otherwise I'll spend my entire time averting my eyes instead of listening to your pitch. And take out most, if not all, face jewelry and make sure your fingernail polish isn't distracting. You've got one shot, so play it safe, for this one day.

Remember, the goal is to get an editor or agent to agree to read more—no one is going to sign you on as a client because of a fifteen minute introduction, but you can hopefully persuade them to give you an email address so you can send them a proposal.

You want to have writing samples and marketing information with you, just in case, and yet be prepared to sell yourself and your book with just your verbal pitch. Bring copies of a professional one-sheet (one page briefly describing the premise of the book, why readers will buy it, similar books, manuscript status, and a brief bio highlighting your writing experience), a one to two page synopsis (short and straightforward, highlighting major plot points), and the first ten pages of the book. If I'm the agent and I'm interested enough in your pitch to ask for a writing sample, don't you think you should have one?

Now. The pitch. Keep it short and succinct. Think elevator speech. Introduce yourself politely, present the hook, the major premise (the conflict and what's at stake), possibly a theme, and why readers will buy this book, and do this in less than three or four minutes. Time yourself. Practice it multiple times. Any longer than this for the initial introduction to the concept of your book and you are up against the tendency of a listener to get sidetracked. This little speech is supposed to be the jumping off point into a conversation, where hopefully they will have questions for you, and you have the opportunity to express what it is you really want to get from this particular meeting, and to go in-depth about your book and your writing background.

If you do get to the point where the agent is giving you feedback on your manuscript or pitch, don't argue. Just listen and nod, politely say thank you, perhaps the old, "Hmmm, that's interesting, I'll look into that," whether you agree or not. Use the feedback to improve for next time.

Almost as important as the content is you. Sit up straight, lean a little forward, speak with enthusiasm (though not high-pitched or at the speed of a chittering squirrel), make eye contact (but don't stare), and project a pleasant, confident personality. Charisma. This is one time you really need to invest all your energy into faking it. The best favor you can do for yourself is to practice the pitch so many times you can say it smoothly and naturally, and then practice the body language I mentioned. Videotape yourself, make sure you don't come across as arrogant or a psycho killer or a monosyllabic bore. If you do, practice some more. Find yourself a couple of real humans to do a test run on.

In the end, just know you need to arrive prepared and not come across as a nut job, allowing the agent to focus on your project. Good luck.

"What does it mean if an editor says to me, 'Sure, send me your proposal' at a writer's conference?"

Um . . . that's a difficult question to answer. The Happy Chip would respond by saying, "What great news! It means the editor liked your work enough to take a more in-depth look at it. Go buy yourself a Guinness to celebrate, make a clean copy, and send it off. "

The Dour Chip would say, "Be proud of yourself . . . but don't go crazy. Editors sometimes do that at writer's conferences because they get fatigued telling people 'no' all the time, or they want to be liked, or they're just too softhearted. Send it, but don't hold your breath—the vast majority of stuff that comes in from writer's conferences sits around for two or three months, then gets rejected anyway."

The truth? Both, most likely. It's great you're getting looked at, so celebrate. But don't be putting money down on that new Maserati just yet.

I was at a writer's conference a year or so ago and had several authors come up to me to say, "The editor at XYZ Publishing said she loves my work and wants me to send it, AND thinks you should look at it for representation!" After hearing that same sentence repeatedly, I finally went to the editor and asked her what she was saying to authors. Her response: "I simply told them the idea had promise, and we'd look at the idea if it came from an agent like Chip MacGregor."

Okay . . . maybe she sounded a bit more enthusiastic when she actually used the words with authors, but I figured out the basic pattern: Editor sounds vaguely positive, author hears the words and turns it into something definitely positive, it gets reported to me and morphs again into something extremely positive. Yikes . . . it made for some awkward moments when I had to explain to people that, even though they considered themselves on the cusp of the next big publishing deal, I was going to decline the opportunity.

Hey, writer's conferences are great. The problem is that writers have paid a lot of money and want some positives—but it's hard for agents and editors to stay positive while basically saying "no thanks." That's a struggle I have at conferences—I want to help writers, but "helping" does not equate to "representation."

Maybe if we all reviewed our expectations a bit, that would help resolve the problem. Because, realistically, a large portion of authors are not going to sign with a publisher or agency at a conference. Regardless, they *will* make contacts, hear a ton of great information and writing instruction, and enjoy getting away from the real world for a short season. They'll go home, put what they learned into practice, and get better. Then, somewhere down the road, they'll get a publishing deal.

"When a publisher requests a complete manuscript at a conference, does an author include the acknowledgements, dedication, and personal author notes?"
Nope. At that point, they just want to read the book. The personal asides can come later—they'll only detract from the larger concept of the story.

"What's the protocol for sending out multiple queries or proposals to agents?"

Hmmm . . . sounds like this must be from someone who had a great experience at a writer's conference! Okay, there's some debate about this from agents, but I'll give you my take on it: I think it's fine to send out *queries* to more than one agent. (Whereas I'd only send out a *proposal* if the agent asked for it.) Sure, if your idea is any good, then every agent would prefer to be the only one looking at your project. But I see no problem with asking more than one agent to look at your work. An agent is going to take your finished proposal and show it to several publishers—why should the agents be treated any differently?

And if you're at, say, a big writer's conference, you show an idea around, and you get several agents asking you to send it to them, my advice would be to spend time talking with those agents. Get to know them a bit before sending them something. You don't want just any agent representing you. This is a business relationship—you want someone you like, someone you perceive as competent, someone you wouldn't mind working with over the long haul.

So, if you met an agent that seemed oily, or there was some guy there who made you uncomfortable, or someone who just didn't know your genre, don't send it. Even if he asked. On the other hand, if there were three agents who you liked, and they all wanted to see it, I don't see anything wrong with talking to all three of them. You're comparison shopping. No harm in that.

That does bring up an odd situation I've seen played out multiple times: Why is it that an agent can turn down proposals from writers all week, but if you turn the agent down, they get whiny? I don't know. I've had similar things with publishers—they've turned down several proposals I've sent them, and never had a second thought about saying "no" to me, but then act put out when they finally make an offer on something and lose it to a better offer from another house. Maybe that's just human nature.

"When it comes to book proposals, should a narrative nonfiction proposal follow the rules for a novel, or for a nonfiction book?"
It's a nonfiction book, so it should basically follow a nonfiction proposal format. But this is a great question, since narrative nonfiction is really a blend of factual writing using fiction technique. Still, you'll find the core of a narrative book is telling a nonfiction story, so stick with the nonfiction proposal model.

"What are some key elements I should include in a proposal? Is there a template somewhere? Are there services that can create a professional proposal for me?"
In this uber-competitive market, you might consider finding a professional to create a proposal, if you can afford it. There are tons of editorial companies online that offer this service—just be sure to research the company. They will, hopefully, know the market, and how publishers think.

On the other hand, it's certainly not necessary. There are dozens of sites online, including blog posts from successful authors and agents, that provide checklists for both nonfiction and fiction proposals. There are also a number of books that cover the necessary elements in depth, including our companion book: *Step By Step Pitches and Proposals: A Writer's Workbook.*

Here are the basics you'll want to include:
Fiction

- The pitch, usually sent in an email or said to an agent at a conference, is a short sales pitch with the hook, the overview, the manuscript status, the readership, and comparable titles. If it's sent in a query letter, be sure to include contact information, and send the proposal document as one attachment.
- A one page writing bio, if you have multiple writing awards or previous publications, and if your platform is something to brag about.

- A one to two page synopsis.
- The first fifty pages of your manuscript, professionally edited; however, your novel must be complete before you submit.

Nonfiction
- The pitch, same as above, though including the unique benefits of your book over others.
- The hook and the premise.
- Manuscript status.
- The take-away for readers (this is important; what solution are you offering readers?).
- Market analysis, including comparable titles, readership, and affinity groups.
- Full author bio.
- Overview of the project.
- The table of contents (for a nonfiction book, the TOC is the most important aspect of your proposal).
- Chapter-by-chapter synopsis.
- Roughly fifty pages of the manuscript, professionally edited.

There's more to say, but this will get you started.

"Does a platform really matter? What if I'm a fiction writer?"

"Platform" matters very much with publishers these days—even for fiction writers. I'm not saying it's the MOST important issue (you still have to have a good story, interesting characters, and solid writing), but I believe we make a mistake when we say a fiction author's platform doesn't make much of a difference. I deal with all sorts of publishers on a daily basis, and I can tell you it definitely comes into play in today's publishing market.

Nonfiction writers definitely need to establish themselves in their topic area. An audience needs to see evidence that you are a credible, timely, and relevant source so they will keep coming back to you. A platform, including a list of published works or an academic website, is essential; "platform?" will be the first question the publisher will have for you.

"What exactly is a platform?"

The simplest way to understand an author's platform is to think of it as a number. How often do you speak? To whom? How big are the crowds? Are you on television? How many stations? What's the size of your audience? Do you have a radio show? How many people are on your database? Who gets the newsletter? How many people donated to your organization last year? How many read your blog? What's the readership of the articles you created for that newspaper or e-zine? Each of those things can be reduced to a number. Add up the numbers, and you have your current platform.

That said, nearly every author can be working to improve their platform. Think of a "platform" as the general awareness of you and your message. The more people you speak to, the more others know about you, the bigger your platform. This is one of the reasons I encourage authors not to spend months creating a book proposal, then follow it with five minutes banging out a bio. You've got to think about how you can impress a publisher with your platform. If you're doing a nonfiction book and you have a small platform, you may need to take the next few months just to build your platform—not just to improve your manuscript.

If you speak at conferences, workshops, trade shows, seminars, business gatherings, and churches, create a list of the places you speak. Where did you speak last year? Where do you expect to speak this year? How many people will hear you? Look through your venues and determine a realistic number. How many more will receive the CD or audio file and hear you? Also think about the demographics of your audience—it can make a big difference to publishers. Who is it that most often comes to hear you? If you're, say, writing a book for teens, it doesn't do you a lot of good to tell me that you're speaking to businessmen at seminars.

Be very clear about sharing all your media opportunities. What radio shows have you been on in the past? What television shows? What is their reach? Who do you have contacts with, so that you are fairly certain you can get on the show again? Obviously you're at an advantage if you've got your own show—even a local show can help. But it's the national media that publishers crave, so let them know about the places you've been and the shows you've done. If you have some sort of club or organization or ministry, you've simply got to be gathering names and emails so you can share that information with your publicist. A database is simply a list of people who already believe in you—so they're already going to be interested in your book.

The writing you do also counts. If you're doing a column in your local paper, or you're writing articles in magazines, or you're regularly writing for a popular website, you've got to share that information. I think one of the most overlooked opportunities for up-and-coming authors to build their platform is through short articles. The growth of the web has created a huge call for content—why not help fill the void? Get your name out there by writing pieces for websites, magazines, blogs, daily offerings, and the like.

I've watched someone like Dr. Dennis Hensley (the guy who runs the excellent Professional Writing program at Taylor University) sell one article a dozen different times. When he was doing a book on time management, he wrote one really solid article that offered good tips on the topic, then tweaked it and sold it to a realty magazine, a management magazine, a business magazine, and numerous trade magazines. Each one was a bit unique—for teachers, he used examples that related to them in the classroom. For restaurant managers, he used examples that involved customer service and staff management. Each audience got good content, and each article was just a bit different. All of those helped create a platform for Dennis.

At the same time, be thinking about how you can use the web to begin creating some buzz for your book. Who could you send it to that might influence others? That's called a "big mouth" list, and you need to begin thinking about how to create your own. Where could you get people talking about your book that might actually lead to some buzz? What sites do readers of your book visit, and how can you reach them?

Randy Ingermanson has begun working with authors facing these types of questions. I think he got tired of writing excellent novels, only to see publishers barely move copies, so he started something called "the mad genius" that is an attempt to help authors build their own buzz. (Google him and you'll see his work.) Of course, you can always talk with a freelance publicist as well, just to see what ideas they have to help you expand your platform.

Here's the bottom line: There used to be a feeling that, as a writer, all you needed to do was to write a great book. That's not true any more—at least not for most of us. You still have to write a great book, but to thrive financially, you've got to think about establishing a healthy platform so that publishers will sit up and take notice.

"What suggestions would you have for an author who wants to write pieces to boost her platform?"

Ask yourself where your potential readers are. What are the sites/magazines/journals/blogs/e-zines where they congregate? What online communities do they participate in? What other author sites do they visit? What companies attract them? Make a list of the top 100 or 200 places where your readers hang out. Then go visit those sites. How does one participate with them? Do they take freelance articles? Are they interested in profiles? interviews? sidebars? numbers pieces? Would they like an interview with an author?

Ask yourself how you can create a piece that fits the site, but promotes you and your book. Once you've figured out where readers are going, and how you can get onto those sites, you write something that's a fit and send it to them.

Put the topic or title in the subject line of your email. Include the piece, give a short bio of yourself at the end, and include links to other things you've written. That will get you started.

Again, the core of marketing is simple: *find out where your audience is, and go stand in front of them.* If you want to boost your platform, that's how you can start thinking about creating some growth.

"I've noticed more authors using the term 'bestseller' or 'bestselling author' in their materials. Is there a rule about this? Must an author make an established bestseller list in order to use that term?"

Absolutely. An author needs to have a book that hits a recognized bestseller list in order to claim he or she is a "bestselling" author. That would mean your book needs to land on a legitimate bestseller list like the New York Times list, the LA Times, the Denver Post, the Wall Street Journal, USA Today, Barnes & Noble's list, or the Amazon Top 100. It's also fine to note that you had a book land in your regional paper—say the Portland Oregonian or the Cincinnati Enquirer, though those lists don't quite have the same cachet as the major lists.

Several outlets (Publishers Weekly, the iBookstore, CBA, etc.) release their own bestseller list every month, and a few track the various genres as well as offering an overall "top 50 titles" in terms of sales. So if an author claims to be a "bestseller" in her proposal, she needs to be able to back that up with evidence of hitting a list.

By the way, BookScan is the reporting vehicle for most bookstores. Many religious bookstores use a different tracking system, called Stats. These are supposed to track book sales by ISBN number, and create a reporting database for publishers. But one of the reasons this can confuse authors is because some books can sell incredibly well and never have their sales reported. Books sold in Sam's Club and Costco, for example, have historically not been reported to any bestseller tracking system—so you could sell 100,000 copies through those venues and never appear on a bestseller list. (That's changing, but understand there are still sales channels that don't participate in the reporting.)

And, of course, books you sell at personal appearances or through your own website aren't reported via any channels. The success of *The Shack* is a good example—the book moved a couple hundred thousand copies through alternative sales channels before any reporting store picked it up and began noting sales, so it had sold a bazillion copies and never appeared on a bestseller list. Once it was trackable, it hit #1 in the religion category. It's reasonable to ask the question, "Would it have been fair for the author of *The Shack* to declare himself a bestselling author prior to making the list?" Maybe . . . but that's not the way the system works.

"You have advised authors to spend some serious cash in order to create a dynamite website. Can you tell me how many zeroes we're talking? And are there templates or places a prospective author could view in order to begin making plans?"

I think a good website can be a great marketing tool, selling your book and, most importantly, yourself. We used to think of sites as akin to a highway billboard—something you drove by, read, and moved on. But now sites are incredibly useful tools—a way to stay on top of the industry, offer articles or tips or blog posts, communicate directly with readers, and let people know about books and speaking events.

Websites have proven to be content-centered—so if you have a plumbing company, you don't just say "great rates and quality service" like you might in a yellow pages ad. With a website, you'll have suggestions for fixing common plumbing problems, a place to ask questions, introductions to the company personnel, a way to schedule an appointment, maybe even a "history of plumbing." In other words, the site has become the repository for information. It's why we've quickly become a nation of readers again. And it's always changing. For instance, MacGregor Literary recently updated our corporate site, we have begun doing more on Twitter, and Facebook, and other social media outlets, and we've updated the software for my blog to the latest WordPress version. Now I'm having people tell me we don't use Tumblr and Pinterest enough, and we could make better use of video. Like I said, it's always changing.

If you're an author who wants to stay in touch with readers (and can devote time to it) your marketing people will probably encourage you to create a good website. And it will mean you can expect to spend somewhere in the $3000 to $5000 range. You can go cheaper, of course (some places offer a do-it-yourself site for $99), but you get what you pay for. And you can spend a heck of a lot more; I know an author who just invested $10,000 in a fabulous site. There are thousands of experts you can talk to about establishing a strong site—there's no reason to have a crummy website any more. If you want to check out author sites, visit some author pages and start clicking. You'll find thousands of authors with a variety of styles and choices to their sites. There are also great templates on WordPress to help you find inspiration.

"While perusing Amazon yesterday, I filtered my search by 'date published' and noticed several pages of books listed for pre-orders due out next year. Is this a sales strategy? Is it common? Is it effective? And how far out is realistic to get a worthwhile response?"

The practice of directing friends and readers to pre-order your book on Amazon has been popular for several years now. Yes, it's a sales strategy, and yes, it has become more popular for the savvy author. Here's why: If you push everyone you know to pre-order your upcoming book, all those orders go into effect THE DAY OF RELEASE. So if you've done a lot of groundwork, and really convinced a lot of folks to pre-order your title, then on that first day it looks like a lot of people logged on and ordered your book. The book gets noticed, your title shoots up near the top of the Amazon rankings, and you hope to get some great word-of-mouth buzz going. Maybe it gains enough momentum that gets it noticed by other reviewers and readers. The rankings on Amazon are all comparative—that is, the Amazon system is constantly monitoring sales velocity, so if a bunch of orders are triggered at once, it suddenly causes your book to look like a bestseller, even if it's just briefly.

As for the effectiveness of this system, it seems to work best for authors who really beat the bushes and convince people to pre-order a book (not an easy thing to do in these days of instant gratification). Store orders are great, but a sudden hit of 2000 books on its release day can really grab the attention of people (and of your publisher).

You asked how far in advance to do this . . . that's a tougher question. I see some bestselling authors working promotion as much as six months out, but my guess is most authors will find this effective in the last couple of months before the book officially releases. In fact, getting people to order in the last thirty days within the book's release might be your best strategy. It's not easy to organize a large group of purchasers like this, though, so be prepared to work, especially if you have little-to-no platform built up.

"Is it advisable to give away printed materials to promote your book —bookmarks, postcards, stickers, posters? My publisher says they don't have a budget for these types of things, but I have author friends who say they are essential."
They're only essential if you have some evidence to suggest they'll help you sell your book. Printed stuff like that used to be all the rage. Nowadays, they may help in certain situations (such as personal appearances or local bookstores), or in national campaigns (having giveaways with every purchase at a chain of stores, for example), but they've largely given way to online marketing efforts. If you have some reason to believe this could be useful, then go ahead and invest in them . . . but my guess is you can find other avenues that will offer more bang for your buck.

"Is there any value in book trailers?"

I've read quite a few comments on book trailers (a commercial for your book), and it seems that authors notice and like them more than readers. Frequent comments by readers fall into the "I like to envision the characters in my head" category versus watching book trailers. There are always outliers, though. You know, the trailer that is so good it becomes viral. Generally those trailers are witty or touch a sentimental nerve and have been created by professionals. So . . . I'm not a huge fan. I tend to think authors who invest weeks of work and hundreds of dollars into a book trailer would be better off looking for another avenue to promote their work.

"I've heard book signings are mandatory, but I've also heard book signings are a waste of time . . . which is true?'

I think book signings are great fun in your hometown, where you can have people show up and point out they spelled your name correctly on the cover. They're also fun if you've got a bestseller and everybody wants to have their picture taken with you. And they're generally good for your ego, assuming some customers actually show up.

Do they help sales? Not unless you're a star, though they can sometimes help create buzz about you, garner you some local radio or TV time, and get some extra word out on your book. As publicists say, any publicity is good publicity. But there are few things sadder than walking into a book signing by accident, only to find a desperate author trying to pump his new work to an empty room. You walked into the store to buy the latest Norah Jones CD, or to pick up a Susan Meissner paperback, or to use the men's room, and here is this pasty guy with a desperate look on his face asking you if you've seen his book on "The History of Mayonnaise." You smile, nod, offer encouraging words, and try to get out of there quick. Put yourself in his position. It's awkward. Pretty deflating. I know, because I've been there. I once helped the ladies at Barnes & Noble stock the shelves, since there was nothing happening at my book table.

My friend Annette Smith tells of having her first book signing. She had written a wonderful book of short stories, called *The Whispers of Angels*, and the store had special angel-wing napkins printed up for the event. They also had enough food for a small army. The good news? She ate well for three weeks, and when they ran out of toilet paper during their Christmas party, those angel-shaped napkins came in handy.

"How can I make a book signing successful?"
As I said, nothing is as soul-sucking to an author as throwing a party and having nobody show up. The fact is, if you want to do a book signing, the first rule is simple: *Don't rely on the bookseller to get people there.* They might send out a flyer, or put it on the company website . . . or they might not. I remember one A-level author who showed up with me for a book signing only to find the staff hadn't been told, there was no signage, and her boxes of books were actually *locked in the manager's office, and he was away on vacation.* True story.

So, like in everything else in marketing, don't rely on someone else to do the work—you do it, and have a plan for succeeding. Some tips:

- Invite people. Again, don't sit and wait for people to show up. Go out and invite them. Make it a party. Tell your family they need to show up. Personally invite all your friends—call them, send them notes, check back with them and get some commitments to be there. Focus on inviting groups, since groups of people will make it feel like more of an event (i.e. invite your co-workers, your neighbors, the people at church, the people at the gym or in your civic groups).
- Remind people. Bug them. Get them to commit to showing up. Events like this are successful if people show up. If they don't show up, you don't have a party; you have an empty room.
- Make it a party. If it's near your hometown, be sure to offer entertainment, those folks can just hang out and talk anytime. Have a theme. Make some noise. Do a reading. Dress up. Ask

the bookstore's event person for suggestions—if you get the bookstore staff involved, they're more apt to act supportive of the event. Two of my authors recently held readings at bars; both events were well attended, not to mention the crowd was relaxed and willing to open their wallets, and the bar staff were happy to draw in customers and be part of something fun.

- Bring stuff to give away. You want to SELL books, but you can give away swag. Bookmarks. Pens. Buttons. I've known people who have had drawings for bigger prizes, advertised widely and well in advance to draw in more people. One author gave away a roundtrip ticket to Europe but you had to be there to win.

- Talk to everyone who comes in the door. As an author, you're most likely an introvert—but at a book signing, you're going to pretend you're an extrovert. Walk up to everybody, smile, thank him or her for coming, and ask his or her name. If you need to, have a couple questions in mind to ask people. Be able to talk about your book without sounding like you're desperate to sell some copies. And by all means, let the bookstore staff hear you say, "If you like this, you should check out these other books while you're in the store." Let's face it, the bookstore isn't doing this to be nice to you—they're doing it to bring in potential book-buyers.

- Have a handler there to manage the line, if there is one, and to chat up people while they're waiting to get you to sign a book. A friendly person who can smile and engage people at a busy book signing is a real help to you. Also, you definitely should not be taking the money yourself. If a bookstore staff is not taking payment for the book, be sure you have someone else on tap to be your cashier. You want to be the artist, not the seller.

- Contact your local TV and radio people. Get in touch with the local arts and entertainment reporter of the paper. Tell them it's a "local girl makes good" story, and invite them to be there. Make sure to build in time for an interview. I also suggest having a short press release prepared so they can use that as a base. Make sure you write it exactly as you would like to see it in the paper, in case they don't follow up.

- Have someone taking pictures. You can use them on your website later, and you can share them with local press. Make sure to get one with the bookstore staff.

- If there's a crowd, read from the book and take questions. If you've invited the local book groups or the local writing groups, they'll want to hear you read a bit, and they'll want to ask about your writing techniques. In a setting like that, read three or four passages from your book, for maybe twenty minutes, then answer questions for another twenty to thirty minutes. Then you need to get to the book signing portion of the night, before people leave without buying a book. Invite people to come talk with you as you sign and sell your books.

- Have candy or cheese for everyone. If possible, serve coffee or wine, since food and drink loosen people up and make it feel like more of a party and less of a sales pitch.

- Again, talk about how great the bookstore is. Mention friends' books that are in the store. Or, if you're doing this at a country club or a community center or a restaurant, make sure to invite the audience to do something there, or buy something, or be involved in some way. In other words, try to get the venue and its staff on your side.

- Get there early. No matter how well you plan, the arrangements won't be right. If you have no idea how many people will show, try to put out only twenty or so chairs at first, keeping it intimate, with your stool or podium only a few feet from the crowd. Have someone willing to add chairs as the crowd grows.

- Dress nice—the rule of thumb is to dress one level above your audience. (So, if they're in jeans, you're in business casual. If they're in business casual, you're in something a bit more formal.)

- Show your personality. Your book reveals who you are, so readers want to see you. If you're funny, show some humor. If you're dark, offer them a bit of mystery. But don't just show up thinking you can sign books, shake hands, and walk away.

People who are coming want to either support you (if they know you) or get to know you (if they're simply fans of your work). They all want to see the real you.

"How can I make radio interviews effective?"
I used to be the host of a syndicated talk radio show, and I've got five principles to suggest . . .

First, *learn to tell your stories briefly*. Radio is fast-moving, and they aren't going to let you tell a five-minute story. Listeners want stories, but they want them quick and to-the-point. So practice beforehand, create short stories that illustrate your points, and then share them with listeners.

Second, *no matter what the host asks, tell your stories*. Look, if you've done a book on "saving money to pay for your child's college education," you pretty much know what the host is going to ask. With every interview, the hosts are going to ask questions about two things: you and your book. So a lot of media trainers will give you this advice: *Ignore the question and tell your story*. As a longtime radio guy, I think that's the best advice I can offer an author. Whether the host says, "Why the interest in this book?" or "Tell me about yourself," or "What's the biggest crisis people are facing?" all they really want is for you to tell your interesting stories and entertain the listeners. So, ignore the exact details of the question and tell your story.

Third, *don't expect the host to have read your book*. Either you or your publisher will have sent the host a series of seven to ten questions to ask in the interview. Some will just go down your list of questions. Others will take it and make it their own. But always remember this bit of advice: *There are two kinds of hosts—those who haven't read your book, and those who don't know how to read*. None of them will have actually read your book.

Fourth, *be friendly, even if the host is a jerk*. Some hosts like to spend the time talking about themselves. Some want to be shock-jocks and challenge you. I once had a terrible experience with a very popular radio talk show host who wanted to keep arguing about Hillary Clinton, even though my book had almost nothing to do with her. If you watch a lot of Fox or MSNBC, you'll find a lot of yelling . . . but that doesn't work well on radio. People simply turn it off. If you want them to remember your book, be winsome. Even if the host is acting like an ass.

Fifth, *understand that most interviews are either five to eight minutes, eleven to fifteen minutes, or twenty-four to thirty minutes long.* Find out which type of interview they're scheduling so you can prepare. The short interviews just want a couple bang-up stories and ordering information. The medium sized interviews want to spice it up with some personal info. And the longer interviews want you to interact with the hosts.

Sixth, *if you can set up your own radio blitz, by all means do so.* You can start between 6:00 and 7:00 AM on the east coast, set up an interview every fifteen to thirty minutes, and move west, where drive time ends between 9:00 and 10:00 Pacific time. That gives you a block of six to seven hours you can fill, back to back. And you can do it again on the drive-home, starting at 4:00 PM on the east coast and going until 6:30 or 7:00 PM on the west coast. I once did that for three days straight, and got nearly a hundred short interviews for my book. (A radio booker charged me $600 to set this up.) It takes stamina (and a strong voice), but gets the word out fast and heavy.

"I've been asked to speak several times since my book came out— some large venues, some very small. My problem is I don't know what to charge when I speak? A flat fee? A sliding scale? Is there some guidance you can give me?"
Happy to begin this conversation. Okay . . . start to think about creating a matrix for your speaking events.

First, there are certain topics you speak about. (We'll name those A, B, C, D.) Second, there are lengths of time you can do each one—for example, let's say you can talk about Topic A for thirty minutes, for two hours, or for an entire weekend retreat, but you can only talk about Topic B in a couple one-hour blocks of time, so you could do a one-hour or two-hour chunk of content—and Topic C is nothing more than a twenty to forty minute casual talk.

So now you have some options . . . you've got A1 (thirty minutes of Topic A), A2 (two hours on Topic A), A3 (a whole day on Topic A), B1, B2, and C1, etc. Still with me? That starts to give you important ways to figure out the topic and time.

Third, you need to consider how many times you speak. If they want you to just show up and give a speech, that's X. If they want you to teach several workshops, that's Y. If they want you for a weekend retreat, that's Z. (This will start to get confusing, but it means you'd be doing a Y Day—several workshops, where you'll do A2, B2, and C1, for example. If you hate my numbering, create your own that makes more sense.)

Fourth, you need to consider the venue. The bigger the venue, the more you charge. Most speakers have one to three tiers (small setting, medium sized setting, large or arena setting). Some only have two tiers, and some have a couple tiers and a retreat setting. And Holly, who spent fifteen years as a speech coach, wants me to add that when you ask about the venue, make sure you ask who will be in the audience and what the controlling organization considers the goal of the speech.

Fifth, and last, you need to make sure they cover your travel expenses. Now when somebody calls you to speak, you or your assistant simply asks a series of questions:
- On what topic(s)?
- For how long each time?
- How many times will I speak?
- How big is the expected audience?
- Where is it?

Once you have those questions answered, it's easy, because you have a grid to use. You just fill in the components, and you begin to see how much work is involved. Now, let's talk money . . .

The key money issue is called base pay. How much is your base pay for a one-hour talk? Let's say it's $500 for an hour, or $300 for a half hour. If you make, for example, $300 for speaking one time, for thirty minutes, to a small group, and you've been asked to speak several times, you just have to map out the extra costs. They want you to speak once to a large group for an hour, then lead a workshop to a smaller group, then sit on a panel. It will take an entire day. And you have to fly to Atlanta to do it. I do some quick math: $500 to speak to the big group, another $400 to do the seminar, maybe $200 to do the panel. So I say to them, "That will be about a $1000, plus you need to fly me coach to Atlanta and put me up for two nights. I think we can do the whole thing for about $1600." They offer you $1200 and you have to decide if it's worth it to you.

I hope I didn't over-complicate this, but that's the basics of how to think about charging. Once you know your base pay, it's fairly simple: topic + time + number + venue + travel = cost.

"As an author, how do I negotiate a movie option for my novel? Do I give a free option? Do I demand money for the option?"

You don't normally grant an option for free—you negotiate the option for the production company to pay you a certain amount of money, for a certain period of time. What the customer is buying is really the exclusive chance to explore turning your book into a movie. They'll talk through the idea, figure out if there's a market for it, how the story might change, who might be possibly be cast as actor or director, what the costs are, etc. And you normally go through a literary or film agent who has relationships with film and production companies, and who can make sure all the details are done correctly.

A note on this: If you think publishing contracts are tricky, just wait until you see a film contract. There are a lot of stories about authors who sold their idea cheaply, then made nothing when the concept moved to the screen. It's called "Hollywood Accounting," and if you're interested in this, just Google the horror story of Deborah Gregory, who created The Cheetah Girls. She made some money on the books, but when they went to the stage, TV, and the big screen, she was promised 4% of net profits… and the accountants have always been able to show there were no net profits. So while the parent company has generated millions in cash from The Cheetah Girls, Ms. Gregory has made nothing. Ouch.

"What's the worst query you ever received?"

This one is easy. All of us have pet peeves—I happen to hate it when an author uses hyperbole and hype to sing their own praises: "This life-changing book will make you laugh, make you cry, make you quit your job and move to Toledo so you worship at my feet." Fer' cryin' out loud—let somebody else sing your praises.

The same holds true for competitive analyses in which the author basically bashes everybody else's book on the topic. Nothing will make you look more like a self-absorbed jerk than to suggest "C.S. Lewis got it wrong but I'm doing it right."

However, the worst query letter I ever received was from some prophecy nutjob in the Midwest. He claimed (and I swear I'm not making this up) he and his son were "the two prophets foretold in the Book of Revelation." He informed me I needed to send him "a contract and a sizable check," and warned if I didn't do so, I was incurring God's wrath. He went on to say I could expect "severe weather patterns" and that God was "going to kick [my] ass." Really. Needless to say, I immediately leaped into action by suggesting he write to another agent friend of mine. Funny . . . now that I think of it, I haven't heard from that agent friend since then.

"What type of interactions with writers would you rather avoid? It must be hard to deal with those that are rejected and upset."

Before I answer this, I want you to understand, I really love my job. I love working with writers, and I am well aware of the time and heart that goes into creating a book. But there are some writers who take their passion too far and make it difficult to walk openly in the publishing world.

First, there is the author who asks you what you think of her novel, says she really wants you to be honest . . . then acts offended if you're not in love with it. I recently sent a very gentle rejection to someone, and her response was to come back and accuse me of being "a phony—just like those other agents who rejected me." Oh. In other words, if you get rejected by a bunch of literary agents, they're all wrong and you're right. And my agreeing with them makes me a phony. Uh-huh. I'm sure she's got a huge future in publishing.

Second, there's the weird guy I mentioned earlier who follows you around at a writing conference and acts too friendly. He always has a bad book idea, feels compelled to tell you about it every chance he gets, and doesn't understand the concept of personal space. It's like being chased by Dr. Weirdness and the Children of Doom.

Third, there's the person who acts like you're her personal assistant. "Here's my novel. Do a review and tell me what to change." Um . . . I don't represent you. You just sent this in cold. Where does it state that I have to respond to your request? The fact that you're a writer and I'm an agent does not automatically mean I owe you my time. I don't even have to respond to your email.

Fourth is the guy who insists on a face-to-face meeting so they can explain their book in person. Merely sending you his proposal is not enough. Why is it bad writers always think their work is going to improve if they can explain it face-to-face? Do they plan to visit each buyer of their book in order to explain their concepts in person?

64

A while back I had a guy call several times and ask for a meeting, eventually mentioning one of my favorite restaurants in town. I agreed . . . basically because I wanted to eat at the restaurant. By the end, his "explanations" did not sway me, nor did the food. And, by the way, if you request a meeting, asking me to invest my time in order to get my perspective on your work, you pay. Kapish?

There are others, but you get the picture. Politeness counts . . . which is an odd thought, coming from me, I suppose. I've certainly used up more than my share of karma being impolite. I'll sometimes be too blunt in an assessment and hurt people's feelings. I'm not doing that to intentionally wound someone. Negative words can be hard to hear. I recently sent a cryptic email to a fellow agent who took it as a rebuke. I hadn't meant it that way; I was simply offering my thoughts. Email can be a tricky thing at times, so be sure you are not coming across as bossy, or condescending, or rude, or entitled, or crazy.

"What do I do with a bad review?"
Someone recently wrote to say, "I got a terrible review on Amazon. I hate even going there to look at it. Tell me, what do I do with it?"

You know, one of the things unpublished authors don't realize is that once you put something into print, it's there forever. If you say something stupid in a book, you're stuck with it. You can go to the person and apologize, but the words are still out there, waiting to be discovered by millions of other potential readers who will never get to hear your personal explanation or apology. Writing is a scary thing. Publishing can be terrifying.

I've often done fairly blunt assessments of books and articles, and, as I mentioned, at times I've hurt people's feelings. But I never set out to do that. I mean, it's not like I saw the book, didn't like the author, and decided to toast them just for fun. When I've said something was stupid or badly written, it was because I was trying to offer an honest evaluation of a project. But that's not universally respected. Let's face it—plenty of people *only* want you to say something nice, or to say nothing at all. (I once said some critical things at a conference about a James Dobson book, and he was so incensed he had his personal assistant call me to complain . . . as though my opinion was so important that it actually mattered to him. Geez.

So, if you're asked to review a book that's awful, what are you supposed to do? Lie about it? It seems to me the best thing to do is to be honest but as gracious as possible, speaking the truth (or at least the truth as you see it), being sure to direct the comments toward the writing and not the writer. But it's not fair to readers if I gloss over the truth.

Unfortunately, a bad review like that can hurt an author's career, to say nothing of the author's feelings. I find when I'm asked to review a book for a friend, I'm leery of putting pen to paper, only writing reviews for books I love. On the other hand, if a magazine or website hires me to do a review, I have to be as honest as possible, even if that means sounding critical or harsh.

Unfortunately, there are others who don't write negative reviews because they are being honest but, instead, bash authors for personal reasons (for example, Amazon does not vet the reviewers, leading to both false bad *and* good critiques—we've seen too many reviews from mothers and friends to accept the glowing evaluations as honest).

So, how does an author get past that type of review? It is imperative to know you *never* win anything by attacking back. A couple of times I've worked with authors who wanted to write in a defense or a clarification after experiencing a bad review. They wanted to go on Amazon and defend themselves. But offering an explanation for a bad review never works. My advice? Forget it. Put the bad review in a box, set it behind you, and move on. We all get bad reviews, we all get some personal attacks, we're all going to face readers or reviewers who sometimes just don't like us, or have some weird axe to grind. That's life.

That's especially true with books, where beauty is in the eye of the beholder. You might write something you think is deep and thoughtful—but a reader might find it silly and turgid. Guess what? That's the life of the writer. If you can't live with it, pick a different career. *Nobody* is universally beloved in this business. There were people who hated Mark Twain, and people who wrote terrible reviews of *The Chronicles of Narnia*. Different strokes for different folks.

Kurt Vonnegut once talked about the unfairness of personal attacks in bad reviews, claiming rage and loathing for a novel is "preposterous. He or she is like a person who has put on full armor and attacked a hot fudge sundae." When you get a bad review, recognize the attack for what it is: small-mindedness, misunderstanding, a chance for the attacker to make himself feel better, or, perhaps most commonly, an honest response to something not suited to the reviewer's tastes. Then forget about it. Go read a positive review to make up for it, forget the bad one, and move on to something else.

"How long do you pursue publication before you give up? Should I have given up earlier? Who knows who-or-what I would have been had I pursued something else all these years."

No one can answer that question for you. Was it worth it to you? Some of this relates to a core principle I preach: *Publishing your book does not validate your life.* Seeing your name in print doesn't automatically mean you are a good person, or that your life has been worthwhile. Who were you writing for? Why were you writing? What did you hope to accomplish? Answering your personal questions should reveal if your result was worth your investment. (However, I have the gift of prophecy, and can reveal to you that, had you not pursued your book, you'd have become a used-car salesman in Arizona.)

"I've been at this writing career for a long time, and feel as though I don't have much to show for it. I've done two novels at a

small house, then two more at a bigger house, but they didn't sell well, so now I'm having a hard time landing a contract. I've enjoyed myself, but I'm not sure the time and effort have been worth it. I love my art, but . . . I wanted more. And I go to conferences and it feels like everyone is having more success than me. Any advice for a writer facing the big question of 'Is all this worth it?'"

I've been agenting a long time, and I've had a form of this question thrown at me countless times (see above). An author signs a deal with a small house and does okay, so she signs a deal with a bigger house and, even though she writes good books, those books tank. Maybe the house did no marketing. Maybe the readership couldn't find her. Maybe the author and publisher didn't know how to work together. There are a million reasons a book doesn't work, but suddenly the author finds herself stuck. She has lousy sales numbers, maybe she can't get a deal, or she CAN get one, but it's back to SmallTimeVille. Hey, it happens. Does she stick with it? Change her name and start over? Try a new genre? Look for a collaborative job? Go back to the drawing board and try to come up with a blockbuster idea? Self publish? Give up?

There's no one answer that's going to fit every situation, of course. And if you hang out at conferences, it *will* feel like everyone else is doing better than you—but they are not, trust me, it's just that so many of those authors are smartly writing their own PR. I love the fact that the writer who emailed me this question was quick to say she had enjoyed the ride and loves to write. Because I think a writer in this situation really needs to look at his or her motivation, and think through goals— what do you want to accomplish? What will constitute success? What will make you happy? Maybe making an appointment to speak with a good agent about career plans could come in handy.

Here is some great advice from musician and writer Bill Withers: "One of the things I always tell my kids is that it's OK to head out for wonderful, but on your way to wonderful, you're gonna have to pass through all right. When you get to all right, take a good look around and get used to it, because that may be as far as you're gonna go."

And you know what? All right isn't always so bad.

PART 3

THE ROLE OF THE LITERARY AGENT

"What does a literary agent do?"

A literary agent helps an author create a proposal and a polished manuscript, has industry connections that will get the author's proposal in front of editors, understands and negotiates contracts, works with the publishing house and client to build marketing strategies, tracks royalty payments, develops new ideas with the author, and discusses writing goals and options, including self and hybrid publishing and other career opportunities.

"How has the role of a literary agent changed in the new world of publishing? Is it still necessary to have an agent?"

I was happy to get this question (and several similar questions) recently because I was at a conference a while back and someone asked this of a panel I was on. As soon as it was asked, I was thinking the agents would jump in and start talking about the changes to our role . . . but then I realized that, on this particular panel, I was sitting with several newer agents, and I don't know if they had the work experience to offer a good response. The microphone was at the far end of the stage, and I listened to four people say, "I think the role of the agent is still the same as it always was."

I sat there, shocked. But after they had responded, I didn't feel I could jump in and say, "Everyone here is wrong!" In retrospect, I should have found a way to say something. You see, I've been agenting for seventeen years now, and my role has changed completely. The job isn't the same as it was when I started. I think every aspect of publishing is in a state of evolution (perhaps a state of revolution) at the moment. The role of authors has changed—they are now marketers and business persons. And the roles of the bookseller, the editor, and the publisher are changing. So it would only make sense the role of the agent would be significantly changed.

I spend a lot of my time talking with authors about marketing and platforms. I spend a fair bit of time talking with authors about their careers, and their indie or hybrid publishing plans. Career and list management, marketing and platform development take up a lot of my day—and were things we rarely discussed fifteen years ago. Sure, I still have to sharpen proposals, meet with editors, show them projects I think are a fit, and negotiate deals, but the role has changed considerably.

Remember, there's no one correct way to agent, just as there's no one correct way to edit or sell or write, but I'd say a good agent is more essential now than ever, now that the playing field is flooded with writers. As I touched on in the previous question, a good agent will:

- Recognize good, salable writing (and help the author focus his or her time on those projects).
- Know the market and have relationships with the people who are decision makers in the industry.
- Be able to develop and package a proposal and manuscript.
- Assist with the overall planning of a career, and offer guidance on career management (including branding and strategic direction).
- Offer input into marketing and brand management
- Know contracts and be able to negotiate effectively
- Be able to sell sub rights, dramatic rights, and foreign rights
- And step in and handle disagreements or say the hard things to editors.

Of course, not all agents do everything (or do everything well). And not every author needs the same thing. One author needs an agent to be a coach and encourager; another needs an agent to be a business manager.

And yes, to answer the question that's the elephant in the room, I think there are times an author doesn't need an agent. As I said in my introduction, I'm not an Agent Evangelist. Some people can manage this without an agent, though they will probably need marketing, career, and technical help. And I think it's only fair to note that nearly every big, successful author has an agent. Even today, in the age of hybrid authors, and with stories of authors making piles of cash on Amazon. For some writers, I'm becoming the indie-publishing career assistant and sometime-consultant, as are all the agents in my agency. I'm not afraid of it—I just think that's the way the role of literary agent has moved.

So . . . can you get published without an agent? Of course you can. You can also sell your house without a realtor and draw up your own will without a lawyer. But you may not want to do any of those things, and it's getting harder and harder to do them well. In fact, trying to get a career established in publishing without a good agent is an uphill climb. It's doable, but it's harder than it used to be. A good agent should help you decide on a salable idea, create a better proposal, and get that proposal in front of the decision-makers who matter. More and more, your agent will help you refine your work, assist you with your marketing, and shape your career . . . not just get you another book contract.

"When am I ready for an agent?"

Here is where you need to be honest with yourself. Where are you at with your writing, both in craft and output? Consider the following:

When NOT to get an agent:
- When you're not a proven writer. Generally, publishers are looking for great ideas, expressed through great writing, and offered by a person with a great platform. Sometimes they get all three, usually they settle for two of three. I've taken on some unproven writers because I liked an idea or the writing, but understand that I have to work MUCH harder for an unknown author, and get less return, than I do for a proven author . . . and that's why agents prefer to work with proven authors.
- When you don't have either a full manuscript (if it's fiction) or a dynamite proposal and sample chapters (if it's nonfiction). Without those, you're simply not ready.

- When you won't let others critique your work. Criticism is how we get better. Why is it the worst writers seem the least ready to listen? Maybe because in their hearts they know they aren't that good? Admitting so would hurt their self-esteem.
- When you're not ready for rejection. This is a tough business. Do you have any idea how many times I hear the word "no" in a week? If you can't take some rejection, or if you can't take criticism, or if you can't take direction, go back to the dry-cleaning business. You obviously aren't tough enough for the writing biz.
- When you have so much time on your hands you can do everything an agent does, plus write.
- When you feel like you're "giving away" fifteen percent of your income. I don't think many of the authors I work with resent my percentage . . . they know I help them earn more than they'd get on their own. But if you don't feel that way, you're probably not ready to work with an agent.
- When you enjoy selling books and negotiating, you know what you're doing with marketing and contracts, you have the relationships with editors to set up your own book deal, *and* you don't mind singing your own praises.

When TO get an agent:
- When you have a dynamite proposal that a publisher will fall in love with. The agent should help you find the right house and maximize the deal.
- When you don't know whom to go to. An agent should have strong relationships in publishing . . . always ask a prospective agent who he/she represents, and ask what deals he/she has done lately. If an agent doesn't really represent anybody, or hasn't really done any deals, they may be new, but if they've been in the game a while, you have to wonder if they're really an agent or just playing one on t.v. An agent lives or dies on his/her relationships. Make sure you pick somebody who is good at relationships.

- When you don't know about contracts (they are legal documents that govern every aspect of your book for as long as it's in print—a contract can impact your life for years) or how to negotiate.
- When you don't know what a good deal is versus a bad deal.
- When you don't know how to read a royalty statement.
- When you don't know how to market your book.
- When you don't have time on your hands and don't want to negotiate with the publisher yourself.
- When you don't want to be the person promoting or selling yourself and your work.
- When you need career guidance.

If these apply to you, then you'll probably find an agent helpful.

"What questions should I ask if I run into an agent in the wild?"

I love this question! Once you know you are ready for an agent, you'll need to know what to ask. The next time you spot an agent in the wild (and they haven't spooked and run) pull some of these out of your pocket:

- How long have you been doing this?
- How many contracts have you negotiated for authors?
- Who do you represent? Would any be willing to talk to me?
- Which editorial personnel have you done deals with?
- May I ask them what they think?
- What sort of authors and projects do you represent?
- What do you like to read? (Ask for titles!)
- Can you give me a book title you sold that you loved?
- Can you give me a book idea you sold that you loved?
- What would you say are your best skills?
- What's unique about your agency?
- What percentage do you earn on a book deal?

- Are there any hidden fees or charges? Any up-front costs?
- Do you charge back all your expenses?
- Have you ever worked in publishing or done any editing or writing? (If the answer is "no," ask yourself if this agent can give you what you need.)
- How do you approach career planning?
- Do you work by yourself?
- Are you full-time? If part-time, is this your main job? Do you have a list of editors you are regularly in contact with?

"And how do I find an agent?"

My advice for *finding* an agent is not a guarantee for success. It's plain hard work and luck that will bring you and an agent together . . . there are thousands of prospective authors per each agent in the U.S.

Your best bet is to try to meet agents up close and personal, to make that connection. The easiest way to do this is to find writing conferences and schedule an appointment with an agent (sometimes you can do this on the website for the conference or you can sign up on location the first day). It will cost you, but look at it as an investment in your career.

You can also try to make appointments at their office or at a local coffee shop, but it can sometimes be difficult to find a phone number or email address in order to establish that contact, and an agent may be reluctant to meet with someone they don't know. These kinds of meetings generally are set up through mutual friends or contacts. Do you know anyone who has contact with an agent? Talk to them.

If you can't set up a face-to-face meet, then your final strategy is the cold call, where you research the email addresses of agents and send out proposals to people who have never heard of you.

You need to make sure your emailed query letter and attached proposal are well written and targeted specifically to the agent you are sending it to (e.g., a romance query goes to a guy who sells romance, a YA manuscript goes to an agent who reps YA authors, etc.).

"What characteristics should I look for in an agent (or what makes a good agent)?"

It's easy to pick a few things ("the ability to spot talent" or "connections to publishers") and declare them to be the essential elements of a good literary agent. But the fact is, a good agent is probably an honest person, with good book experience, who brings to bear the talents you need. It's hard to select a good literary agent if you don't know what you need help with. So before selecting an agent, do some type of inventory. What do you need in an agent? An encourager? An editor? A person to talk through ideas with? A contract negotiator? A spokesperson? A life manager? A financial and career advisor? A marketing maven? If you have some sense of what you need, you'll be better able to figure out what characteristics to look for, and how to select the right literary agent for your own career.

"How important is it to consider industry contacts/relationships when deciding on an agent?"

In my view, "experience" and "connections" are two of the most important things a good literary agent can bring to most clients.

If the prospective agent hasn't worked in the industry, he or she may not understand the economic of the book world. If they haven't done a bunch of deals, they may not understand what makes a good deal, or what's important in a contract. If they don't have connections with editors (and particularly with editors in your genre), they may not be able to best help you shape your proposal, or be able to get it in front of the right people.

This is why I'm always trying to clarify with people what I do, and do not, represent. If somebody has a children's book, even if it's a fabulous children's book, I'm the wrong guy for it. I don't sell children's books. And even though I'm pretty well-known in the industry, I don't have relationships with the editors you'd need to know in the world of children's publishing. Oh, I might be able to figure out who to show it to, and I have a good enough reputation that the editor may choose to review the project. But I'm honest enough to admit I wouldn't bring any cachet to the situation. Nor would I know how best to improve the manuscript, or maximize the deal. It's just not my area of expertise.

So, yes, contacts in the industry are essential for an agent to do a good job representing you in today's publishing market.

"I heard an agent speak at our writing group. He sounded interesting, so I went to his website. You have to contract with his agency for a year and pay an up-front fee of $195, though it's not clear if that is per project or for all your works. Is that the usual course?"

Yikes. Several thoughts come to mind . . .

First, don't go to any agent that asks for an up-front fee. That screams rip-off. I don't know of any credible literary agent who asks you to send him or her a check right off the bat. You can't be a member of AAR by charging fees, and you'll get listed in "Predators and Editors" if you do. Stay away from fee-based agents. If you're interested in researching this topic further, I highly recommend the book *Ten Percent of Nothing*, which offers a fine exposé of scam agents.

Second, like I've already said, you don't want to sign up with an agent you know nothing about. Websites are marketing tools, and some of them over-promise, when in reality the agent will under-deliver. I can claim anything I want on my website (that I'm the best agent in history, that I'll make you a million dollars, that I look exactly like Brad Pitt), but if we don't know each other, and if we've never met, how in the world do you know what to believe? Be cautious over sites that over-promise. (For the record, I look exactly like Brad Pitt. Especially if you stand far away. And squint. And are blind.)

Third, be wary of agents trolling for business by sending you advertisements. It's one thing to meet someone at a conference, or to begin a dialogue over a submission you've sent in—most of the authors I represent are people I met somewhere and had a discussion with, or they were introduced to me by current authors I represent. I think that's true of most agents. What you're describing is akin to a lawyer chasing ambulances. Sorry to sound negative, but this sounds like a scam.

"I noticed you were critical of agents who sell services to authors. I approached an agent I met at a conference to discuss my book. He rejected it for representation, but said they had an editor who could work on it, and I paid about $700 to the company. They still decided not to represent it, but when I self-published it on Amazon, they offered to help me with the marketing, again for a fee. Is that wrong?"

Here is the official wording from the Association of Author Representatives: "Members pledge themselves to loyal service to their clients' business and artistic needs, and will allow no conflicts of interest that would interfere with such service."

Turning a potential literary client over to an editor who works in-house at an agency is bad business—I'm either an agent or I'm an editorial service, not both. The guidelines go on to state: "The AAR believes that the practice of literary agents charging clients or potential clients for reading and evaluating literary works (including outlines, proposals, and partial or complete manuscripts) is subject to serious abuse that reflects adversely on our profession. For that reason, members may not charge clients or potential clients for reading and evaluating literary works and may not benefit, directly or indirectly, from the charging for such services by any other person or entity." (There is an exception for agents who get paid for evaluating a proposal through a writing conference, since writers go there specifically to get a formal evaluation of their work.)

I have frequently said to potential authors, "This needs a good edit—here are some editors I like." But I don't have any financial tie to those editors, nor do I receive anything back from them for sharing their info with writers. AND the guidelines also note that, "Members may not receive a secret profit in connection with any transaction involving a client." So no kickbacks are allowed. Holly Lorincz works with me, and also owns her own editorial business. I don't profit from her editorial services, nor do I have anything at all to do with her client list or the projects she agrees to take on. Her business is completely separate from mine. She's a good editor, so I don't hesitate to suggest her name to people who ask me for references, but I'm always quick to say, "And her editorial company is not tied to MacGregor Literary in any way."

The problem here is the potential to scam authors . . . in essence, to say to a writer, "I don't believe you're good enough to be my client, but you can pay my editor to fix your book, then maybe I'll consider it. No promises, but thanks for the cash." That's wrong, according to the AAR, of which I'm a long standing member. Things are changing, and agents are doing more than they used to, but trying to make money directly from their authors by selling them services is not kosher.

"Can you explain how an agent gets paid?"
Happy to explain this. When I complete a deal for an author I represent, I'm paid a commission. That's the only money I make. Traditionally, when it was time for the publisher to send money, they would send the entire amount to the agent, who would then deduct his or her commission (the standard is fifteen percent) and send a check for the balance to the author within ten days. This was the system in

place for years, and many agencies still work with that system. The strength of it is that the agent knows the author has been paid, and paid the full amount. This is pre-tax money, so at the end of the year the agent would send a 10-99 form to the author, detailing how much money was paid.

When I started working as an agent seventeen years ago, I was working for Alive Communications in Colorado, and they used a different system—divided payments. With that system, the publisher cuts TWO checks. The first is sent directly to the author, for 85% of the deal. The second is sent to the agent, for fifteen percent, along with some sort of evidence that the author has been paid his or her amount. To my way of thinking, this was a smoother system. The author got paid faster. There was less bookkeeping for me. I didn't have to fill out the 10-99's. And, most importantly, I would never get a phone call from an author saying, "Hey, you big doofus—the publisher says they sent you my money two weeks ago! Where's my check?!" I've found too many fights in business occur over money, and I prefer the authors I represent feel as though we're on the same side, and we have no reason to fight over money. When I started my own company eight years ago, I decided to keep in place the "divided payments" system.

Both work. Neither is better than the other—they're just different. Which is good, because I've occasionally heard other agents say that not everyone will do divided payments. But in my years of doing this full-time, I've had exactly *one* US publisher refuse to cut two checks (it was a fine small publishing house in New York, and the woman who bitched and moaned about it retired soon after that deal was done). Few of the foreign publishers want to be bothered with cutting two checks, so if your agent is doing foreign deals, that money will most likely be paid to the agency and forwarded on to you.

Back to getting paid: Publishers used to pay your advance half on signing, half on delivery. Now most pay a third on signing, a third upon delivery, and a third on publication (with the people at Random House fighting to pay a quarter on signing, a quarter on delivery, a quarter on publication, and a quarter when the book flips from hardcover to trade paper . . . sigh . . . another sign of the apocalypse—they'll soon be asking for a quarter to be paid upon the CEO becoming eligible for social security, no doubt). Of course, an advance is recoupable against your royalties, so with each book sold some money is credited to your account. You earn back your advance with royalties, then when the book earns out the publisher starts setting your money aside and will send it to you either quarterly or semi-annually, depending on your contract.

"A publisher requested my manuscript at a conference. They later sent me an evaluative memo with some editor notes and a request that I rewrite it and send it back. Is this worth mentioning in an agent query?"

Sure it is. Understand that many editors will request a proposal at a writers' conference. Unfortunately, many times they aren't really "requests." They are more "resigns"—as in, "The editor was resigned to saying yes to every author who showed them a proposal." That's because the bulk of editors, while exceptionally nice people who know their jobs, are also big weenies. They hate looking you in the eye and saying, "no, that doesn't fit us" or "no, this isn't ready" or "no, did you stop taking your medication?"

Consequently, as I mentioned earlier, I'll often hear authors tell me an editor requested a proposal, when in actuality the editor did nothing more than agree to look at it later, so as to reject it later, by letter, thus saving himself from having to tell the author "no" face-to-face. (Okay, I'm exaggerating. A bit.) However, if the editor has taken the time to review your work and make notes, then has suggested you do some revising and resubmit, that shows genuine interest. So, yes, I'd tell a prospective agent that bit of news. I hope that helps.

"I was just offered a contract on my novel. Since I don't have an agent, should I seek one at this point? Would it be better to have the agent simply review the contract for a fee?"

There's quite a debate about this issue. I know several agents who would say, "If you already have an offer—call me!" I mean, they'd be happy to get fifteen percent for a deal they've done no work on. But I have some doubts about the value of that type of situation. Let's say you got a contract offer featuring a $10,000 advance. If the agent steps in, he or she takes $1500. Is the value of their work worth that? You can ask a contract service to review your contract for around $500. (However, be careful . . . there are good and bad authors, good and bad agents, and good and bad contract review services. Make sure to ask questions, so you get someone who knows what they're doing and has done it before.) A contract service won't negotiate for you or improve the deal—they simply evaluate and report back to you. So if you have a bunch to negotiate this may not be your best choice.

You can also talk with an intellectual property rights attorney, but be cautious—they're generally paid by the increment, usually by the six-minute increment for every phone call, email, conversation, or reading you ask them to do. It can add up fast. A good attorney can certainly help, and should be able to strengthen the contract. But in my experience you want to be careful who you're working with—I've had too many situations where the goal of the attorney seemed to be nothing more than to keep the clock moving (though I expect some attorney will come onto my website and claim that never happens). The longer it takes them, the more they are paid. I know of several authors who ended up paying more to have a top-flight entertainment lawyer review the contract than they were paid in advance dollars. Yikes. Generally speaking, your family lawyer won't have enough experience to really help you with a publishing contract—the guy doing grandma's estate or your last real estate closing probably doesn't know much about current publishing contracts.

As for getting an agent, I would say you want to make sure the agent actually does something to earn the commission. He didn't help craft the idea, didn't help you polish the proposal, didn't shop it to editors, so ask what exactly he's going to do in order to bring value. Review the contract? Negotiate better wording and royalties? Assist with marketing? Shop your dramatic and foreign rights? Handle potentially sticky situations? Help with long-term career advice? Assist with other services, such as helping you self-publish your backlist?

I've often had authors come to me with offers in hand, and I've frequently told them to pay for a contract evaluation, since it's less money. I have sometimes agreed to take on an author, but usually for a reduced commission (if I didn't help with the project, I don't know why I'd take the full fifteen percent.) And I would encourage you to think long term—Is there someone you want to work with? Is there an agent you like and trust, who can help you with your career, and not just this book deal? A good agent may be willing to take less in order to work with you.

My advice: I don't think it's fair for me to take the full commission on a book I didn't sell, but not every agent out there agrees with me, so talk with others and solicit some opinions. And, whoever you are, congratulations on getting the book deal, by the way.

"I have an agent who I signed with six months ago. Is it fair for me to think he will respond to my direct questions? (Questions like 'Who did you send my proposal to?' and 'When did it go out?') Those don't seem unreasonable to me, but he never responds. Is there something about the relationship I'm not understanding?"
Agents are just people, and they come in all types. Some agents keep in touch regularly. Others choose to stay away and only show up when there is news. I'd suggest that a good agent should keep an author apprised of where you are in the process, but perhaps the two of you could simply have a discussion and clear up how each of you work. Certainly neither of those questions you mentioned are unreasonable.

It's your manuscript, so you should know who is seeing it. It would not hurt to call and have a chat with your agent about expectations.

"I signed with an agent, but wasn't happy. I fired that agent, and moved on to another. But now my first agent is claiming anything I ever talked with her about is her responsibility! She claims that if I ever get a publishing deal for the projects she once represented, she is to be paid the agent's commission. Is that legal?"

This is another concept I can't fathom. I understand getting paid if I've done the legwork. Let's say I've worked with an author to develop a project, showed it to publishers, and started to get some interest. If the author hears about the interest, fires me, then approaches the same publishers to try and get the deal and save themselves the fifteen percent commission, I should still get paid. I state in my agency agreement that if I'm working with a publisher on your behalf, I'll still get paid even if you fire me and do a deal with one of those publishers I was just selling your work to. But I've seen the situation you're describing a few times lately—an agent claiming that if you *ever* sell the book they represented, they'll still get paid. I'm not a lawyer, so I cannot give legal advice, but I would think this would be awfully tough to have stand up in court. If you've moved on, tweaked the proposal, time has gone by, and you're now talking with new publishers, I don't see why your previous agent would demand payment . . . but I know some agents will do exactly that. My advice: Read any agreement carefully before you sign it. If the agent has a clause like this, that's incredibly restrictive, ask to have it altered.

"Can an agent help me plan the marketing for my book?"

Normally an agent will help you think through some of the marketing, maybe even help you plan it or oversee pieces of the marketing plan. But a literary agent is different from a publicist or a marketing manager. As the author, you are most responsible for marketing your book, so don't leave that up to your agent, your publisher, your sales staff, your publicist, your mom, or anyone else. You are in charge of marketing.

Nobody knows the book better than you, nobody has more invested in it, and nobody is more committed to its success than you. A good agent should be able to help with the plan, and should certainly ensure that the publisher is doing what they promised. Your agent might even help you map out a strategy beyond what the publisher is doing. But most agents aren't going to do the actual marketing or publicity work on your behalf. There's no way to make any money doing that, and it's the domain of the author... or a freelance marketing or publicity consultant.

"Do most agents sell movie rights?"

Yes and no. I *have* sold dramatic rights; my experience is that most of us will sell them, if we get a call. But it's more of a reactive thing than a pro-active thing—that is, they're waiting for the phone to ring. I know of very few literary agents who actually have relationships with people in Hollywood, so most wouldn't have the first idea who to call in order to sell your dramatic rights. Movies are just a different world. It takes a different set of relationships to make that happen effectively.

"How important is it for my agent to be knowledgeable about the specific genre I write in? For example, let's say I want to do a New Adult series, and my agent says she knows nothing about NA. Should I be concerned my proposal won't get the right treatment from editors?"

Agents tend to work in certain genres, thus making connections with editors who work in those genres, and develop great relationships with people and publishers.

So, yes, it's nice if you can work with an agent who has relationships with editors in the genres in which you write. That said, most agents are also willing to grow their business. If you came to me with a really good proposal for a genre I've not worked before, I would admit that to you, and either say, "You might want to find another agent to do this one,"

87

OR I might say, "You know, this isn't a field I've done much work in, but I love this proposal—let me do some research, make some calls, and I'll come back to you so we can develop a plan."

I have a good reputation with publishers, so they'll talk to me if I bring up a new project... the issue is more "can I actually land that deal with a publisher if it's in a new genre for me?"

"I've been contemplating getting an agent, but I've also thought about starting my own publishing company. What are the biggest rewards for each?"

The biggest rewards for starting your own publishing company would be that:

- You're the boss and can make all the decisions.
- You'll make roughly three times as much money on each book sold.
- It's faster to do your books yourself.
- You have creative control.

And, of course, the downside is that you have to do it all yourself. Some people love running a business, others couldn't run a business if their life depended on it.

The biggest rewards for working with an agent would include:

- Having an experienced person offer counsel on things like contracts and negotiations.
- Having someone make introductions to you with both foreign and domestic publishers, as well as with subsidiary companies like movie people.
- Having someone with specialized knowledge assist you in your career, your marketing, your covers, your brand, etc.
- Having someone encourage you, as well as having someone plead your case for you when there's a problem.

- Having someone who knows the business be able to seek out new opportunities.

I suppose there are other things (editorial help, concepting, titling, etc.), but those are some of the first things that come to mind. Again, I'm not here to serve as a commercial for literary agents—I think most of the authors I represent feel I provide a good service for them, but I understand why some authors want to go another route, and that's fine.

"What attitudes are career-killers for writers looking for an agent?"

"I know it all." "I don't have to listen." "I can't write now so I'll wait for my muse." "My work is better than those schmucks selling books because it's Great Art."

"Will you consider representing self-published works?"

I'm happy to look at a project that's been self-published. Everyone in the industry is looking for a writer with a great idea, a great platform and great writing, and a book that's been self-published is no longer a deal breaker for publishers—they'll just ask the author to turn over their erights. If the book has done pretty well, the publisher understands there is a market for that particular title.

But the fact is, the thing I've found that's missing most often in a lot of self-published books is great writing. We see a lot of good writing, a lot of OK writing, a lot of so-so writing. But great writing is the very first thing I look for in a self-published book, and I frequently don't find it . . . which could be why the book wasn't picked up to begin with. In saying that, I'm not slamming self-published books. The fact is, I know of several excellent writers whose books were not contracted by publishers.

But, overall, that's a problem we have in the industry—a lot of self-pubbed titles that are badly in need of a strong edit. So, if you are trying to grab my attention, edit, edit, edit.

"What are the three most important things agents look for in a query?"

A strong writing voice, clarity of argument (if nonfiction) or story (if fiction), and an author platform. Short and simple answer, but true. Creating a pitch, and writing a query letter and proposal, takes time and thoughtful crafting, as we discussed earlier.

"How important are queries to your agency?"

I use them as ways to explore talent. Of the queries that come in cold (that is, not introduced by editors or authors I already represent, and not someone I spoke with at a conference), the percentage of queries that lead to me taking on a client for representation is very low.

"What five things guarantee a query has a quick trip to the trash bin?"

Grammar, spelling, and punctuation errors. An author promising me this book will be a blockbuster, or that God told them to write to me. Weird fonts and formats. An arrogant attitude (particularly people who don't want to listen to advice). Sending me poetry and other stuff I don't represent. For instance, I just got an email that read, "While I know you don't normally represent poetry, I thought you might be interested in my epic poem about . . . " Um, yeah. Because making your poetry *longer* is sure to get me to love it.

"I sent a query to an agent months ago with no response, not even a rejection note; when can I send a nudge note?"

Where is it written that an agent must respond to you just because you wrote to him or her? Answer: it isn't. An agent isn't obligated to respond to everyone who writes him or her. Frankly, it's physically impossible to reply to the majority of unsolicited queries. I've got a job to do, and time is money, so I really can't take the time to read every project somebody sends in cold. I don't feel that's a dereliction of my duty—I simply don't believe I owe every writer a favor. I state very clearly on my company website that I'm not looking for unsolicited proposals. Still, people send them. I also state on my site that I don't have time to read every project coming in over the transom, and that I don't return unsolicited proposals, even if they come with a postage-paid envelope.

It's just not my job to take responsibility for someone else's idea. And yet, I have people I've never heard of write to complain that I didn't respond, or that I didn't return their materials—as though their decision to mail me something puts a burden on *me*, merely because I work as a literary agent. Wrong. I generally represent people I know— maybe we met at a conference, or often they were a referral from a current author. But it's a very rare thing for an agent to yank something out of a slushpile and offer an agency agreement.

So, make sure you have realistic expectations. You very likely will not get a response if you are sending in an unsolicited manuscript. Now, if you've been asked to send in the complete manuscript after a meeting at a conference, that's different. Give the agent two to three months to work through their piles of stuff, and then send a kind, short note asking if they had a chance to look at the work yet. Include your original pitch, to jog their memory, and re-attach the manuscript, just so it's all available again.

Try not to get frustrated if you still don't hear back (though you should hear something at this point), but feel free to continue shooting out queries to multiple sources unless you receive an offer for representation.

"How much does an author platform play into your decision to represent an author?"

For nonfiction, it's the first question I'll be asked, so it matters. And now I'm starting to be asked that question of fiction authors. You have to mention it in your nonfiction query—and it can't hurt in a fiction query. As I've already stated in this book, a "platform" is just a number—how many people read your blog? how many read your articles? your newspaper column? how many hear you speak at conferences? how many listen to you on the radio? how many are you connected to through Pinterest? through your organizations? through [fill in the blank]? Those are all numbers. Add them up, and you have your platform. And here's a hint: the bigger the number, the happier the publisher will be.

"What are agents really looking for with fiction?"

That's a huge question, of course, because I can't speak for all the agents. But here's a thought: The best fiction I ever read *moved* me. I was never the same after I read Tom Pynchon's *Gravity's Rainbow* or Gabriel Garcia Marquez's *One Hundred Years of Solitude* or Leif Enger's *Peace Like a River*. I love to pick up a novel and feel changed by it. It's a rare event. Too many novels seem to be exercises in angst ("I've had a hard life!") or narcissism ("Look at me!") or merely creative crap ("I'm going to try something completely different, just to show you I can do it!"). They don't move me toward knowledge or emotion or growth. But that's what I'm always looking for—a novel that moves me, that leaves me changed. I think every agent is on the lookout for the "wow" moment, when some writer's work smacks them as fun, moving, fresh, and well-crafted.

I'll give an example . . . A couple years ago, I was approached by a young woman from New Zealand who wanted to show me her romance idea. The story was okay, but the writing was fabulous—fresh, fun, with great voice. We worked on the project, she changed the story, and I just sold Kara Isaac's novel to an editor at Simon & Schuster. I could repeat that same story numerous times, with authors whose work I fell in love with: Lisa Samson, Susan Meissner, Gina Holmes, Jenny B. Jones, Mark Bertrand, Les Edgerton, Ann Tatlock . . . Their work appealed to me right out of the gate, was fresh and well written, and they had strong voice. That's the answer, in my view.

"How do agents and editors feel about an author writing under a pseudonym?"

No law says you have to publish under your legal name, but it's not like it was in the old days, before the birth of cyber stalkers. It is nearly impossible to write under an assumed name and sustain the illusion for long. Some authors have created social media sites under that fake name, using a fake photo and fictional biography, but that just makes it worse when the author's real identity is discovered by some twelve-year-old computer genius who will out you on his Twitter feed.

Granted, there are some good reasons to write under a pseudonym. It used to be, publishers would only publish one book a year by the big authors, which is why Stephen King was also writing under Richard Bachman, so as not to flood the King market. (Of course, that publishing strategy is long dead.) There are also those authors who have awkward names. Destiny Hooker? I can see why that author chose not to put herself in the sights of the late night comedians, especially when she was writing serious books on couples therapy.

The biggest reasons these days, though, is that authors will try to repackage themselves after they had a couple of books tank (a decision a publisher will likely get behind if the author is still on contract), or if well-known authors are jumping genres and need to build a different fan base. This last is probably the easiest to sustain, since these authors generally are open about their pseudonym, having fun creating an alter ego to go along with the assumed name, and engaging in social media with tongue in cheek. The readers are usually in the know, and like taking part in the facade, while still feeling like the two lines of books are totally separate. Nora Roberts is famous for her contemporary romance novels, but she also does exceptionally well as J.D. Robb, writing edgy romantic suspense. Davis Bunn is another author who was firmly established as a gentle romance novelist but assumed a pseudonym to publish edgier works. Both have created a separate stream of faithful readers in each of their genres.

For most authors, I recommend using your name, or a version of your name. Today's readers really want connection. They want to know what you look like, what your backstory is, to see what you have to say on Twitter or Facebook, maybe even have a chance to have a minor exchange with you on one of your social sites (though, with any public interaction, I urge you to always consider your audience—you want to tantalize them, not offend them to the point they go away). This is hard for shy or private people, I know, but fan sites are bigger than ever, and they are important to feed . . . no one can help you sell books like those fans on the ground.

"Should Christian writers look for Christian agents?"
I'm being asked this question because I've represented a lot of Christian fiction over the past decade. My answer really depends on why you are asking this question. Well, okay, I take that back . . .

If you are asking because you believe Christians should only work with people of the same faith, my answer is no. Do you seek a surgeon who shares your faith before doing back surgery, or do you try to find the person most qualified to work on your spine? Do you insist your mechanic sign a statement of faith, or do you just want to find the guy who can fix that irritating rattle in your Subaru? Because if you are suggesting values and specific spiritual beliefs dictate the people you will engage with in this world, especially in the business world, then you have a sad, limited worldview. Don't get me wrong; I'm not suggesting you ignore the fact that your literary consultant has a pentagram tattooed on his forehead. You should like the agent, and be able to work with him or her, but it doesn't matter if they are going to your

94

version of heaven or not. You just need to know they can read your material and get behind it, that they believe in the quality of your manuscript, and are willing to try their best to sell it. Besides, if you are waiting around for an experienced agent who works solely with conservative evangelical publishers, it may be a long wait . . . it's slim pickins.

Now, if you are asking because you think an agent really needs to understand the Christian market in order to sell to a Christian publisher, then you are right. But only partly. Because a competent agent knows a variety of markets, from religious nonfiction to general market sci-fi. Of course, agents tend to have most of their publishing house connections in only a handful of areas, but there is no reason an agent wouldn't know people in both CBA and ABA markets. You simply need to do your research. Did the agent you are considering sell inspirational-literary fiction, which you happen to be writing? Then, yes, this person will probably be a good fit, regardless of the other markets they work in. But would you give your spec-fiction novel to an agent who had never sold in that genre, just because he attends church on Sundays? I doubt it. Competency and trust are what you want in a literary agent.

"How do agents work with hybrid authors?"
Here's how I see myself fitting in: I'm a multi-published author, a former publisher, and a longtime agent. A hybrid author often needs help with the technical side of things (reading contracts, setting up release schedules), the business side of things (dealing with editors, arranging to get the vendors paid), the selling side of things (contracting foreign rights, talking with Hollywood producers), and the marketing side of things (crafting a marketing plan, connecting with a magazine on a press release). Most importantly, a hybrid author needs an experienced person to go to for career advice. A good agent will probably offer some practical help with several of those issues, and free you up to focus on your writing.

95

If you have more questions in this area, please see *Part 5: Hybrid or Self-Publishing*.

"How much do agents deal with publishers after a contract has been signed?"

This is a great question, and gets to the heart of a good agent versus a bad agent. In my view, a bad agent is someone who is only there when there is money to be made. I've seen agents say things like, "If you are offered a contract, call me." What a stupid thing to say. If you're offered a contract, that agent doesn't have to do much. You've already concepted the book. You wrote it without any advice or direction from the agent. You shopped it to publishers. You got an offer. Now the dipstick wants to swoop in and take fifteen percent for what—reading the contract? That should be illegal.

Look, there are no two author/agent relationships that are the same. I have authors who want to talk through their book ideas with me, and authors who don't give a rip what I think of their ideas. I have authors who want to be part of every contract discussion, and authors who say, "Chip, just negotiate the contract and tell me when it's ready for me to sign."

There's no one right author/agent relationship. It's going to depend on the personalities and the needs of the people involved. But I can tell you that once a contract has been signed, the agent's job is not done. He or she needs to ensure contract compliance (Did the publisher pay? Was the amount correct? Does the author need to talk through the manuscript? Is the book done correctly? Is it on time?). The agent also should be involved in the pre-release planning, offer insight into things like the cover, the back cover copy, the interior design, and the marketing of the book. He or she should be the author's spokesperson when there is a problem. The agent sticks up for the author, takes their part when the difficult discussions have to happen. Most of all, the agent is there to talk through career choices, so this isn't a one-book career.

My doctoral program at the University of Oregon was in Policy and Management, with an emphasis in organizational development—how an organization develops over time. I had a graduate teaching fellowship at the Career Planning and Placement Office, talking with grad students who were getting degrees in the arts, helping them map out a career plan. When I got into artist management, my focus was not on "getting the next contract," but on "helping the artist develop a long-term career." In my view, that's the role of your agent. The contract is important, but that's just the beginning.

"If you had to choose between one or the other would it be a gifted writer or a popular social media personality?"

This one is easy for me to answer. If I could wish for authors to work with, it would always be for gifted writers, not for celebrities. I've worked with a bunch of celebrity authors over the years—music people, TV stars, sports personalities, and the like. Many of them get attention, since they are known quantities in the world of media. But I am, at heart, a words guy. I'd rather see a great artist create a fantastic story through words than watch some celebrity wave at the camera. In the long run, it's the art that will last. I believe in the power of words to change people, and ultimately to make a better world. (At heart, I'm really a hopeless romantic.) So, while I'm happy to talk with someone who is famous and who will land a big book deal, it's rarely as satisfying as discovering the great new talent who is going to create a life-changing manuscript that we'll all love.

"Do you ever tell anyone they do not possess a talent for writing?"

Not often. But yes, I have, and it's always hard. And sometimes I just have to say, "This isn't marketable, I can't really do anything with this. It's not a fit for me. And it's not ready for Prime Time. Sorry." Think of this as on par with singing talent—if the person really can't carry a tune, or has no sense of rhythm, at some point they need to hear someone tell them, "You can't sing—there's no career here. Please be realistic and have fun with this as a hobby. But let me suggest you get off the stage and look for something else." Truth can be helpful, but it can also be painful.

PART 4

DEALING WITH
PUBLISHING HOUSES AND EDITORS

"What is the process of getting your proposal selected by a publishing house?"

Okay. First, think of a publishing house as being an actual building. Your proposal probably isn't walking in the front door. More than likely, it's sliding into the building by way of a window known as an acquisitions editor (often an acquaintance of your agent, sometimes a person you met at a conference, or maybe a guy who lost a bet). He or she will read through it, make some suggestions, talk it over with your agent, and eventually make a decision on whether or not they think it's worth pursuing.

Most publishers are relying on agents to do the initial filtering of junk, so the slush pile has sort of moved from the publishing house to the agent's office . . . which means you're probably going to have to sell it to an agent first, therefore adding one more step to this process.

Once it's actually in the building, if the acquisitions editor likes it, he or she will take it to some sort of editorial committee, where they sit around grousing about their pay and making editorial jokes. ("I'm having a DICKENS of a time with this one!" "Yeah, let's catch a TWAIN out of town!" Editorial types love this sort of humor. That's why they're editors and not writers.) Eventually they'll run out of bad puns and be forced to discuss the merits of your proposal. If it's a nonfiction book, is it unique? Does it answer a question people are asking? Is there a perceived market for it? Does the writing feel fresh and offer genuine solutions to the question that's posed? If it's a novel, does the story have a clear hook? Is there a well-defined audience for it? Does it feel new, or as though it's a story that's been told a million times? Most importantly, does it have Amish people, zombies, or a spunky girl with a heart of gold? If the whole package passes muster, it moves to the next step . . .

The publishing committee is a group generally made up of folks from editorial, marketing, sales, accounting, and administration. They'll meet somewhere between once a week to once a month, depending on the house, and they'll have an agenda of books to talk through each time, with the various representatives offering their own perspectives—the editors will talk about the merits of the words; the accountants will figure out the costs and potential dollars in play; the sales guys will begin discussing who they can sell copies to; and the marketing people will sit around complaining about why they shouldn't work on *this* one, since they've got so many *other* things to do. The group will talk about the market for the book, if it fits with the rest of the books on their list, what the author's platform offers, what it would cost to print the book, what the marketing costs would be, and how many sales they think they could generate. This is the group that will explore the feasibility of doing your book. They may send it back to the acquisitions editor to do some more work.

At that point, the editor has to run a Profit & Loss sheet, or pro forma, in which they'll take wild surmises as to how many copies they can expect to sell in the first year, what the hard costs of ink/paper/binding will be, what they'll spend on marketing, and how much money they'll have to throw at the money-grubbing author, who, if she really loved words, would write her damn books for free, since we know the publishers are only in it for the joy of reading and to serve humanity. The editor will take this information back to the publishing committee, who by now has had all sorts of time to think up new reasons why they shouldn't do the book. They'll talk about it again, this time with hard numbers attached. Eventually the pub board will be forced to make an actual decision, so they'll probably throw the Urim and Thummim, make a sacrifice to the gods, maybe dig out an Ouija board, and decide on your book.

I've heard people say there are a series of "sales" to get to this point. The author sells the agent. The agent sells the editor. The editor sells the editorial team. The editorial team sells the pub board. Once that group makes a decision to contract the book, they have to negotiate a deal, then put it on a list and make it part of the process—because the sales guys are going to have to sell it to retail accounts, who in turn will attempt to sell it to the reading public. It's a lot of work. And all of that points to one thing: *It's tough to get published.* Each step along the way is an investment, so even the books they say "no" to have had dollars spent on them.

A publishing house has these filters in place so they can do the easy thing and say "no" to you. (Really. That's the reason they exist.) The purpose of the process is to say "no" to most everything. Therefore, if you want to be published, create proposals they can't say "no" to. Of course, that's easier said than done, but that's the basic idea—work on your proposal so it piques their interest, provides a clear hook, and answers any objections. If you do that, your proposal, and then your manuscript, is much more apt to be selected by a publishing house.

"When someone is hired by a publishing house and allowed to acquire new books, are they trained? Do they acquire individually or as part of a team?"

An acquisitions editor has usually spent time with the company and has a feel for what he or she should be acquiring. Most are brought up through the system. They know if the company does well with historical novels, or if they like self-help books, or if they struggle to sell memoir. So most acquisition editors know the list and the company culture—and yes, personal tastes will shape the books they bring in. If an editor likes thrillers, and is charged with building the list, you can pretty much expect his or her preferences will begin to be reflected in the books they're doing. (Though not always—an editor at Harlequin is generally responsible for acquiring romantic novels, no matter how much she happens to like spec fiction . . . again, knowing the corporate saga and culture is essential.) Editors shape houses. That's the way it's always been in publishing. So a publishing house that hires a bunch of new acquisitions people gets reshaped by the editors who work there.

That said, few editors (just a handful of executive editors) have the authority to simply go acquire. The system looks like this:

Step one is that the editor must like the presented idea. He or she works with the agent and author to sharpen the proposal and make it as strong as possible.

In step two, the idea is usually taken to the editorial team. In this meeting, the merits of the book are discussed, several people read it, the team evaluates it, they determine if it fits the corporate identity, they explore other factors (such as "is this book too similar to one we did last season?" and "don't we have enough Regency romances already?") and try to determine if the entire team feels they can get behind the book. They may ask for further changes, they may reject it, or they may decide to continue the discussion. If the team likes it, the project then moves on to the next step.

Step three is yet another committee, known as the publishing board, or publishing committee, explained in the previous answer. Eventually this is the crowd that will decide to publish something. Or not.

So, the decision to publish a book really doesn't reside with one person. It *starts* with one person (an editor, who is the champion for the book and essential to the process), but the decision is really made down the line, by a much wider group of people. That way they can all take credit for the project if the book hits the bestseller list, or blame the editor if the book tanks.

"Do I need to be a tough guy, or make sure my agent is a bulldog, when it comes to contracts with publishing houses?"

A contract isn't a fight where somebody has to win and somebody else has to lose. Think of it as being a way for us to get our agreements down on paper, so that we both are clear as to what will happen in the various scenarios. If you begin by looking at this as a fight, you've set yourself up for problems.

One of the places where agents and publishers have to force themselves to be polite is during contract negotiations. I'm used to simply handling this stuff as business—I don't get terribly emotional about it. There are notes to work through and discuss, so I go through them, point by point. If, for example, I think an author is getting treated unfairly by a publisher because of some contract clause, I'll say, "This doesn't work" or "No other publisher is asking for this." And it'll be the truth. But I've noticed, particularly with certain companies, some editors get personally hurt over negotiations—as though my criticizing something in their contract is an indictment of them personally. It's dumb . . . but it happens. I have to remind myself to be extra-nice, even though this is just a business discussion, not a reflection on anyone's character.

Anyway, politeness still counts. The successful editors and agents and authors have, by and large, figured this out.

"What's some of the big picture stuff I should be asking when I look over a contract?"

This is a list I use when mentoring agents on reading contracts:

- What is the goal of this contract? In simple terms, a contract should ensure that the more books are sold, the more money you make. You can talk with your agent or a contracts person about how that plays out, but the more copies the publisher creates, the cheaper they are to print. That means there is more money coming in on each book—and you, as the author, should share in the reward.

- Who gets the copyright? As you look over your contract, make sure the copyright is in your name. You're not really "selling" your book to the publisher—you are granting them a license to sell your book to others. You created the book, and you still "own" it.

- What are the royalties? Most general market publishing contracts will pay your royalty based on the retail-selling price of the book. The standard hardcover royalty scale in ABA is

10% on the first 5000 copies sold, 12.5% on the next 5000 copies, and 15% thereafter. On the other hand, if you're doing a CBA contract, you'll generally find that royalties are paid on net (that is, you're paid a percentage based on the amount of money the publisher received for each book).

- How soon will the book release? Most contracts state the publisher will release your book within twelve to twenty-four months after they receive the manuscript. That date keeps stretching out farther—not because the publishers wants to wait, but because production, marketing, and sales are requiring more time. Publishers are now creating catalogs twelve months out, which means there is significant pressure to make sure they get the manuscript in time to edit and produce it by the ship date.

- Is it important I read the fine print? Absolutely. One large publisher used to offer what looked like fair royalty rates, but in the fine print it noted that if they sold the book at a greater than 50% discount to stores, they'd only pay the author a half-royalty. That led their sales people to tell retailers, "Hey, I can give you 55% off, because that allows us to not pay the author as much." It meant the publisher made more money by giving the greater discount . . . but it also meant the author got the shaft.

- What protection should a contract offer me? Your contract is the final document upon which all decisions will be based. If everything falls apart and you go to court, the lawyers will be pouring over your contract. And a word of caution: I've dealt with at least one publisher whose contract language stated, "If we ever get sued, the author has to pay the legal bills." Yikes! Don't agree to it—the publisher is your partner in this venture.

- What if there is a disagreement about the manuscript? Some contracts will state that the publisher won't pay completion money until they deem the manuscript acceptable. That's fair to a point, but it means they either need to define "acceptable," or they need to offer a mechanism for fixing the manuscript to make it acceptable. I certainly don't expect a publisher to be on the hook for a bad manuscript, but an author who pours a year of his life into a book needs to be given some time to resolve the problem areas in his manuscript.

- What will make me look stupid? Talking definitively about things you don't know about. For example, there is a common myth out there that every author needs to demand cover approval. Rot. Unless you're a marketing expert, why insist on this? I've had deals blow up because an author insisted on a particular cover, even though everybody involved thought it was hideous and would hurt sales. You've already learned to let the expert editor work on your words . . . so let the expert cover artists work on your covers. Admit you aren't an expert at everything. It's fine to expect your publisher to ask your input, but don't set yourself up as an expert when you're not one.

- And one more note: Over the past couple of years, we've started to see some publishers insert a clause that says, "We're planning to publish your book, but if we change our minds, we don't have to pay you anything" or "If the market changes, we can cancel the whole schlamozzle at any time." Fight this. The clause is terrible. Look, either this is a contract or it's only good intentions. Either this is a legal agreement or it's a collection of possible ideas. You would not sell your house to somebody who said, "Okay, I'll pay you what you want for your home . . . but if, any time before closing, my husband decides he doesn't like the drapes or paint, I might call the whole thing off." A contract is a contract—make sure both sides are committed before signing.

"I've just received an offer from a publisher. They want to give me a two-book deal, but I don't know what I'd write for that second book. What do you suggest? Help!"
You raise an interesting point. Some writers would love nothing more than a multi-book deal, knowing it's going to keep them busy for a year

or three. But I've known writers who hate multi-book deals, since they have to live with the pressure that "more books are due." But here's the thing to keep in mind: A publisher is offering a two-book deal because they believe in you. They don't want to turn out a single book and allow it to be orphaned. They want to help you create a career, so they're planning to do this book now, and that book later.

For most of authors, that's a good thing. And I'm surprised they're willing to allow that second book to be untitled. We used to see a lot of those types of contracts, but any more publishers are asking for a detailed description of what that second book is going to be. It's protection, so they know you've got some basic idea of what you'll write next. My advice: If you like the publisher, and feel you've got more books in you, agree to the two-book deal (and then consult a developmental editor or writing coach for help storyboarding a new idea). If you aren't sure about the publisher, or if you think this may be the only time you write in this genre, you may want to ask if you can just make this a one-book deal.

"What clauses in book contracts have proved the most troublesome for authors?"

- Watch your grant of rights. You should be granting *specific* rights, not "everything, always, under any circumstances." If you don't grant it to the publisher, it's retained by you, the author.

- Some publishers have wonderfully easy-to-read contracts. Others have contracts that read like they were written by lawyers from Mars. If you don't understand what you're reading, get help. Options include (1) talk with someone who evaluates contracts for a living and ask for a contract review—it's often relatively inexpensive and money well spent; (2) hire an agent who knows contracts; or (3) if you don't want to give up a portion of your deal, check to see if you'll be money ahead to simply hire a contracts lawyer and have him or her go through it for you and make suggestions. (Again, I'll offer this warning: *do not* hire the lawyer to negotiate it for you. The clock will be running the moment he or she picks up the phone. Just get their suggestions and craft a response letter to the publisher using those as your outline.)

- Read your contract carefully to see if you're responsible to create a chart, bibliography, index, and map of the stars' homes. Your contract shouldn't have a bunch of boilerplate filler, asking you to create stuff that has nothing to do with your book. For example, many companies include an index in their boilerplate language. If you're doing a novel, you probably don't need an index. Suggest they excise that.

- If your contract calls for an "acceptable" manuscript, make sure it offers some method of reaching acceptability. One small publisher I can think of is known for refusing to "accept" a manuscript until they have the cash on hand to pay for it.

- The copyright should be in the author's name, not the publisher's.

- When will the book be published? Keep it within a reasonable window (not "within five years," as a contract I looked at recently proposed).

- Check and see when the advance is paid. Most books are half on signing, half on delivery. But more and more we're seeing publishers try to push out any cash flow —so it's 1/8 on signing, 1/8 on the outline, 1/8 on rough draft, 1/8 on revised draft, 1/8 on editorial revisions, 1/8 on the next full moon, etc.

- Here's a tough question: What's a fair advance? What's a fair royalty? If you don't know, you need to talk with people who do. Attend a writer's conference, rub shoulders with experienced authors, and figure out what's fair. (And a caveat: Don't take one person's opinion as gospel.)

- Check to see what the subsidiary rights are. If you're doing a novel, be wary of handing over dramatic rights since, in my opinion, most publishers are not in the habit of either (a) doing movies, or (b) reverting those rights.

- Say "NO" to a publisher's request for POD rights. In short, it means as long as they have a copy available on a disk somewhere in the universe, so that somebody, somewhere, can someday order a copy of your book, then the publisher can still claim they have it "for sale." Publishing on demand is not the wave of the future; it's simply a way for a publisher to maintain control of your book.

- Get paid as often as possible. If your contract calls for once a year, ask for twice a year.

- Check your author buy-back discount. If you have a venue for selling books, this can make you a lot of money. (And the publisher is *still* selling them at a profit.)

- Be very careful in allowing the publisher the ability to sell or assign your contract. That means the deal you signed with Acme Publishing may turn into a book with Arnold's House o' Titles.

- Check your indemnification clauses. I've seen contracts that ask the author to pay for everything, including the lawyer who happens to be chosen by the publisher.

- Define what "out of print" means. (It's simple: the publisher is no longer selling your book. Don't muck around with other stuff—we had a publisher once claim they still owned a bestselling title because they had a library audio version of the book in print.)

- The option clause: Make sure you know what you're signing. In days of yore, Thomas Nelson had a clause that made an author promise them two books for every book they wrote . . . which meant with every book you did, you were farther in hole! (For the record, I *love* working with Thomas Nelson. They're some of the best people in the business, so I'm not criticizing the current structure at all.) You don't want to get stuck somewhere, unable to do another book, because you've got some involved option that is preventing you from moving forward.

One last thought . . . In a perfect world, you'd get a perfect contract. But we don't live in a perfect world. So, while it's cool to read that you should never, for example, have a cross-collateralized contract, sometimes a new author with no track record simply can't get what he/she wants. That's life. Do the best you can, but don't ask for the world . . . unless you've earned it, of course.

"How much is too much when it comes to brown-nosing your editor?"

Be professional. It's great to send a Christmas or birthday card, perhaps even a box of chocolates or a small gift card on holidays . . . but maintain professional space. Be polite and grateful in emails, but keep emails short, positive, and to a bare minimum. And never call just to say hi. Editors are overwhelmingly busy and do not have time to reply to inane chatter. Keep your distance unless you are working on a project together, or have an important question, or you are ready to query about a new manuscript—and if you have an agent, that needs to be left to the agent.

"How can I tell if I'm working with a good publisher? What makes a bad publisher?"

I think the notion of what makes a "good" publisher is pretty simple: they sell your book, keep in touch, and send you money on time. Oh, sure there are a bunch of other things you like to see in a publisher— helping you improve your work, investing in your marketing, creating a fabulous cover, getting you onto CNN . . . but in the end, most authors are happy with their publishers if they move copies of the book, send the checks in a timely fashion, and stay in touch so the author has some sense of what's going on.

The thing is, this doesn't always happen. Even a good publisher, someone I've worked with dozens of times, can mess up. They can forget to keep in touch, or have an editor leave so that the project falls between the cracks. They can be late on a payment, due to an address change or a foul-up on some detail. Most of all, we can have a great book, and get wonderful marketing opportunities, and still see the book not sell, thus leading the author to believe "the publisher just isn't working very hard on this project." That might be totally wrong.

I once represented an incredible book—the author was a big star, had hosted a TV show, won Grammy awards. The publisher arranged all sorts of media, including getting the author on all the national morning TV shows and the cover of major magazines. Still, the book didn't sell. It wasn't a bad book, but for some reason it didn't hit. That happens. If this business were easy, we'd all be millionaires. In that case, the author decided the publisher was at fault. I must admit, I thought the author was dead wrong. They'd done everything possible to make that book successful. It never really got moving. It never hit a bestseller list. It never sold 20,000 copies. Were they a "bad publisher"? Not in my view. Not any more than the author was a bad writer, or I was a bad agent. Sometimes projects hit, and sometimes they don't. I suppose it's easy to point out when a publisher does a bad job—they promise marketing and don't deliver, or they give the impression that they're going to get a book into multiple languages, or get the author onto major media. The thing is, I've been at this long enough to know that even very well done projects can fail. That's the business. What you want is a publisher who does their best, keeps in touch, sends you checks on time, and works with you on marketing.

A bad publisher is easy to spot. They don't tell you the truth. They say one thing and do another. They are late with the checks. But the fact is, I don't know many publishers who are bad people. Most of them want to do well, and sell books, and make you money. Remembering that this is, at best, an uncertain industry, can help you maintain a sense of perspective. There are no sure things in this business, even when *you* are certain a book is a no-brainer. You'll do best if you keep that in mind, and focus on working well with the editor and publicist assigned to your book.

"In a nutshell, what's the difference between CBA and ABA publishers? And how do I know where my book fits best?"

CBA is the Christian Booksellers of America, a market dealing in faith-related titles, books for and about Christians. The American Book Association publishers encompass everything else, what's known as the general market. There are a tiny handful of books that crossover into both markets (e.g., *Left Behind, The Purpose Driven Life, The Shack, etc.*), but historically (and, even more so, currently), that crossover appeal is rare. Very rare. Secular readers trend away from books with a faith-based or theological message, whether it is fiction or nonfiction, while Christian publishers know they can sell books to Christian readers which pertain to their lifestyle and beliefs. Neither side is very often willing to risk putting money and time behind a book that doesn't squarely fall into their purchasing group.

We could discuss for days the societal reasons why such lines have been drawn in the sand, but regardless of your thoughts on the subject, this is the reality. If your book has a character who talks about God or church or scripture verses, or is sweet and clean and revolves around salvation or grace, or if it provides guidance through the words of Christ, it's a CBA book. If your book discusses living healthy while on the Paleo diet, this is a general market book.

I know a lot of confusion stems from literary fiction, where one or more characters may be struggling with spiritual issues or are churchgoers. *A Prayer for Owen Meany* comes to mind here, which I'd say is definitely general market—John Irving offers up his main characters involved in theological musings, but he is not saying if you believe *this*, then you are saved or redeemed. He shows life, and religion, to be messy and chaotic and not necessarily stable. His characters live in a gray world, which is often a landmark of literary works, showing God-fearing protagonists struggling with realistic problems, like affairs and drugs and abortions—but those are issues clearly portrayed as evil in CBA fiction, which also tends to be more gentle and rarely so gritty. Again, I'm not saying that's how CBA books should look, I'm just saying that's how it is in today's market.

112

"I just completed my first manuscript. Although my self-help book has an underlying religious theme, I would like to publish this as a general market book for the purpose of reaching out to more than just Christian readers. Would this be recommended or not?"

Without having read the manuscript, I'm going to guess . . . no. Secular readers may come to a religious book on their own, but for you to push a Christian-based theme purposefully in the general market, readers will pick up the book, see the word "God," put the book down, labeling you as a proselytizer, and your content message will be ignored. (Which is exactly what many Christian readers do, eschewing any book or music not deemed Christian enough, so don't for one minute think I'm trying to support either viewpoint.)

And, of course, that will only happen if you are published by an ABA publisher, which is highly unlikely. This sounds like a book that supports the Christian faith while also touting another message. If it is well written and inspirational, a religious publisher is your best bet.

"Have you run into situations where smaller publishing houses offer very small advances with a higher-than-normal royalty? What's your take on a deal such as this?"

Sure—most of the new micro-publishers that got started doing ebooks over the past six or seven years do exactly that. They pay a small advance, or perhaps no advance, but offer a 50% net royalty—twice that of legacy publishers. The risk is that the guarantee is smaller; the reward is that, if the book does well, the author can make more money.

Of course, larger publishers will explain that they have an advantage in terms of reach and marketing, while smaller publishers will tout greater author control and a bigger percentage of the take. Every business decision like that is a risk/reward equation. You have to be comfortable with the decision.

"I've seen contradicting opinions in regards to using blog content in books . . . If I write a blog, does a publisher consider all content "published," and therefore unusable in a future book?"

If you write a blog post and stick it on your website, it has, in fact, been "published." But no, that doesn't preclude you from using that material in a future book, assuming you own it. It's just that a publisher won't want to do a book that contains 100% published blog content, since that's already been out there and is available for anyone to read for free. Instead, the publisher will probably tell you they want somewhere between 30% and 70% "new" content in the book. For example, while preparing *this* book, which just happens to be based on my long-running industry blog, we've included newly written entries, excerpts from media interviews, and questions and answers from workshops I've taught, as well as a slew of new questions from various sources (like that lady at Starbucks the other day who overheard me talking to one of my clients and approached me to ask if big publishers will sign a contract with an un-agented author. I wrote down the question and told the eavesdropper to buy my book. I was not nearly as polite to the guy who tried picking my brain at the urinal.

By the way, if you write an article and sell it to someone else's site, or to an e-zine, you may in fact no longer own the rights to it, and then you'd be unable to use it in a book. Make sure to check your contract before using pieces you've sold to others.

"Do editors at large houses ever look at the books at small houses and pick them up? What would get the attention of a larger publishing house?"

It's rare for an editor to look at the books at small houses with the intent of picking them up. Once a book is contracted, it tends to remain at that house (which is why you want to be careful of contracting your book at some small, ineffectual house). It happens occasionally, but almost exclusively because the book has busted out in a big way, or the author is suddenly famous.

When I was a publisher at Time-Warner, we were doing books with several TV preachers (Joyce Meyer, Joel Osteen, etc.). I noticed there were some other famous TV preachers who were gaining a large following, but who had done their books at a very small press. We approached that publisher and bought out the contracts for those books, in hopes of getting backlist titles for up-and-coming TV personalities.

So, it happens . . . but it would be a rare instance for an author to approach a big house to suggest they buy the rights to their book from a small house. The only reason you'd do it would be because your book is going nuts and the small publisher can't handle it, or you've suddenly landed a measure of fame that requires a larger publisher to maximize.

"If I have a growing platform and a number of 5-star Amazon reviews, how do I make the leap from a small, internet-based publisher to a larger, traditional publisher?"

That's a fair question, but you may or may not like my response . . . You either sell a boatload of books and say to a publisher, "See? I can sell a lot of books!" (which may mean you don't need the publisher, anyway . . . you can just self-pub and make the money you need), *or* you put together a great book and proposal, get an agent who believes in you, and approach publishers with it.

But, um, I have to tell you that publishers and agents tend to be less than impressed with five-star reviews on Amazon these days. Too many have been generated by the author (or the author's best buddies, or the author's mom and aunties), so they aren't genuine. They're nice, of course, but no publisher buys your next book because your last one got a pile of five star reviews. They need *this* book to be great. (And, of course, the first thing they'll ask is, "Can you tell us about that growing platform you mentioned?")

"Why don't publishers share their in-house schedule for the book with the author?"

I can't speak for your publisher, but at most major houses, they create a publishing schedule so that you would know when your book is going to release about a year in advance. The book is going to require marketing efforts and a sales plan that will be created months before the actual book is printed. Your house should be sharing this information with you; it's only hurting you both when editing and production deadlines come as a surprise.

"I think writers can still sell books without agents, especially to smaller houses. What's wrong with starting with smaller houses?"

My response: Absolutely nothing. I started at small houses. I still do plenty of deals with smaller publishing houses. In fact, I think nearly all of us start small and move to bigger things. That's how a career (any type of career) is built. As to whether or not you can actually sell your book to them—that's up to you. Maybe you can. But we live in a society that's getting more and more specialized, and that's making it tougher to survive in this business without professional help—at least when it comes to traditional publishers. Even smaller houses like knowing a manuscript has been vetted by an agent.

"What's up with small presses?"

A very strong trend in publishing these days is the growth of small presses, including those who only provide ebook versions of novels. Publishing is going through a huge transition, and with change comes new opportunity. Some new, smaller houses can be more nimble, and they are rushing to create books aimed at the new audience of readers who prefer pulling out their Kindle or iPad to going to Barnes & Noble and buying a printed book. Some of those companies will survive, some will no doubt see great success and become large corporations (that are

116

perhaps no longer as nimble), and some won't make it through next month. At the same time, we're seeing large publishing houses make a commitment to ebooks and new media—even if it may not be as quick or as complete as some writers would like. But the sprouting up of new companies is a good thing for writers.

"How do you evaluate the amount of an advance offer?"

Every major publisher produces a profit-and-loss form (called a P&L) when they acquire the project. Again, the P&L includes ballpark sales projections, generally with a high and a low number. It also includes an educated guess at what the hard costs of the book will be (paper, ink, binding, art) and may include overhead and/or a preliminary marketing budget. Most important, it will tell the publisher what the author can expect to earn from the project. The advance is based upon the P&L, and is heavily weighted toward author earnings. So, if the publisher does the math and thinks they can sell about 5000 copies the first year, at $22 per book, with author earnings of roughly $11,000, they're probably going to make an advance offer of about 70% of that figure, or $7500.

"What are the top ten things about authors that drive publishers nuts?"

- "Here is my thirteenth email of the day for you."
- "I can turn this manuscript in the first of August, but I need the book out by the start of my conference in October."
- "I know my due date is today . . . but is next June okay with you?"
- "You're not doing enough marketing on my book."
- "Since they're having a pub board meeting today, I thought I'd send you my new proposal. I need to know the decision right away, since my life/health/family/career/TV show is riding on this."

- "My best friend told me this is a fabulous idea. She's a cook at our local junior high."
- "I would *never* allow you to include [fill in the blank] in my contract! I don't know exactly what that is, but I read on the web that it's not cool!"
- "I know my contract is for 70,000 words, but I'm turning in 125,000." [Note: you can also insert the number 22,000 at the end of that sentence.]
- "You want to edit this? But . . . God gave me these words!" [Note: You can also change this to read, "That's the cover? But I was envisioning an all black cover!"]

"How much of marketing a book is the publisher's department, and how much is the author's responsibility? It seems like publishers used to do more marketing."

It's funny, but authors tend to think there was this perfect situation in days of yore, in which the hard-working writer turned in her manuscript, then sat back and watched the publisher market her book to the masses. Um . . . I've worked in publishing for a few decades now, and I don't know if that scenario was ever true.

In my view, the first part of the perfect marketing situation is this: The publisher likes the book, gets excited about it, and really markets it hard. I don't see that happen a lot—sometimes, but not a lot. I mean, I'll often see an editor get excited, and I often see hardworking publicists trying to make things happen, but to have the entire company get behind something is fairly rare. The publishing industry has become much more of a celebrity-driven/bestseller-driven industry than it used to be, and publishers spend the bulk of their marketing time working on books they know are going to be winners. Publishing is an 80/20 business (that is, 80% of the profits come from 20% of the books), so publishers tend to go the safe route, pushing the new book from last year's bestselling author, or focusing on the books by people with big author platforms. That's just good business, so that particular plan doesn't bother me one bit.

When *Publishers Weekly* did their year-end report on nonfiction bestsellers recently, I found it fascinating that seven of their top fifteen authors have huge built-in marketing platforms. (That list included Bill O'Reilly and others who have TV shows or serve as television commentators.) That says something about the importance of an author having a platform. But don't miss the second part of what I consider the perfect situation: The author had to work to develop that platform. None of those people just woke up one day and found themselves hosting a TV show—they worked hard to get there. And that's what an author has to do in this era of media-driven publishing.

So, in my way of thinking, the best thing a publisher can do is to acquire books they really believe in, insist the sales and marketing people read them (you'd be surprised at how often they don't), and decide to push hard on certain books. And the best thing you can do as an author is to politely say "thanks very much" for everything the publisher is doing, then go work as though all the marketing is your responsibility. Because, in my view, it all comes back to the author's work anyway.

Yes, there are cases where a publisher decides to market a book so hard that they push it onto the bestseller lists. The old Time-Warner Book Group did exactly that with a couple titles—Nick Spark's *The Notebook* and Elizabeth Kostova's *The Historian*. Neither author was well known at the time, and with both books the publisher got the manuscript in early, had everybody read and get excited about them, created a lot of buzz, and determined to drive the books onto the bestseller lists. But that's rare. In fact, a publisher will only choose to do this process (it's called a "make-book") once or twice a year. And there's no guarantee it's going to work (we've all watched expensive ad campaigns flop). So the lesson is clear: Author, invest the time to build your platform. Take on the marketing of your books. Approach this as a business, educate yourself, and do the hard work to become known.

119

"What should you do if your publisher doesn't have adequate resources for marketing and promotion?"

Um . . . okay, here's a suggestion: Before inking that deal, ask some questions and find out what sort of marketing effort your publisher is going to make on your behalf. I'd say more than half the books released every year have zero marketing efforts planned for them.

Ask some basic questions: What are some of the things you're planning to do in order to sell books? How have you promoted similar titles in the past? Will there be ads? Will you be sending out review copies? Will you set up a blog tour? Will radio talk show hosts be contacted? Will you use postcards or bookmarks or shelf-talkers in stores? Will you be buying online ads? Do you plan signings or a broadcast fax or in-store promotions? Will you commit to doing extensive web promotion? Do you expect me to walk around Central Park with a sandwich board?

I won't bore you with sob stories, but it's hard to find an author who is satisfied with the marketing their publisher did for them. I suppose they're out there, but they are rare. Many authors feel they were promised the moon, then handed something considerably less. At the same time, it can be hard to find a good freelance publicist. They are out there, but they're busy—a professional who has the contacts and know-how to actually help an author get the word out. It's why some authors will swear by one publicist or another. They had a good experience, and they want to duplicate it with their next book.

So, if you're working with a publisher who apparently doesn't have the resources to support your book, you've got a choice to make: Do you let this book die because the publisher doesn't want to get behind it, or do you decide to promote it yourself? (Hint: if you're self-scoring, the answer you want is the latter.) It could mean spending your own money. It will definitely mean doing some looking around to find somebody who has the know-how, the time, and the reasonable budget expectations to help you. I realize this isn't what you were hoping to hear, but this sort of question faces authors every day. I've been talking to a friend just recently who has a book releasing with a major house, but they've had some staffing changes and seem to have forgotten all the conversations they had with the author about marketing her book. She's faced with two crummy choices: Leave it in the apparently incompetent hands of the marketing dimwit she's been handed, or invest her own time and money to try and make something happen. She's choosing the latter, since she's already put a year of her life into researching and writing the book, and she'd prefer to not see it die a quick death.

Still, that's a hard choice. There are a million ideas an author can use to try and market his or her own book, and it means doing a lot of research to figure out what the right choices are—who the audience is, how to best reach them, what methods will be effective in getting the word out to the most people possible, etc. You can quickly spend a fortune on ideas that won't generate many sales. In her case, she's going to contract with a freelancer to (a) get review copies into the hands of those most likely to help her, (b) connect with radio hosts in order to get her booked onto every talk show in America because she's a great with interviews, (c) query magazines and e-zines about the author creating short articles and sidebars that will support the book, and (d) give her some guidance on web ads. Fortunately, she ran out of money before she could implement (e), which consisted of the words "have the marketing director whacked." However, the author will be working on her own to set up dozens of blog tours, she's doing a mailing and email blast of her own to loyal readers and those interested in her topic, and she's jammed her schedule with speaking venues to help her promote the book. It ain't perfect, and it's a lot of work... just like everything else in this business. Welcome to the world of publishing.

"What sort of marketing would you suggest to an author? And what sort of marketing would you most like to see?"
I'd suggest some field research—who is the audience for your book? What's the best way to reach them? (If the answers are "everybody" and

"beats me," you're screwed.) Next, I'd start checking out the creative ideas people are using on the web. Internet book sales exceeded the sales at brick-and-mortar stores last year, so focusing your attention on web-based marketing is a no-brainer. It's the place to buy books. That means it's probably time you took a fresh look at your website, your online videos, your blog, and anything else that sounds vaguely connected to Al Gore's wonderful invention.

As for what I'd like to see? I can think of dozens, but here are two . . . Many publishers have forgotten about radio. But it's on all the time in our culture. People have their radios on at work, in the car, in the kitchen. And it's *free* to listen. It's also cheap to advertise. I'd like to see more publishers figure out how to effectively promote their books via radio.

A second area is one that authors could work harder at: articles. There are newspapers, magazines, and e-zines all over the world, and they're all looking for content. A magazine is a monster that must be fed. Yet I don't see authors taking their work and reshaping it a dozen times, for a dozen different e-zines, in order to get the word out about their book. It's probably the most under-utilized marketing method out there. If you've written a book on "how to be a great mom," you could take your info and craft a couple dozen articles. Each venue gets a unique story to tell, you get great press, and if you're lucky, you'll often get *paid* for the effort. Why won't most authors do this? Because it means a lot of work, and let's face it . . . most of us are basically lazy. But there you go—two responses out of twenty I could have tossed out.

Of course, I'd also like to see publishers give away more copies, since I think it seeds the market. I've never understood why this has gone out of vogue. Publishers claim it's too expensive—but that 176-page trade paperback that sells for $10.99 in the stores only cost the publisher $1 to produce, so giving away 200 copies would only cost them two hundred bucks. Giving away 100 ebooks costs them almost nothing. Yet they'll fight over this, arguing, "it will cannibalize sales!" Rot. Publishers see cannibals everywhere. They've been watching too much Tarzan.

The thing to realize is that, if you're the author of the book, then *you* are most responsible for the marketing. You. Not the publisher, not the editor, not the marketing director. You. So read up on the topic of marketing. Buy some good books and educate yourself. Attend a marketing seminar. Look for unique ways to sell yourself and your books, rather than duplicating what everybody else is doing. You'll find yourself an expert in no time.

PART 5

HYBRID OR SELF-PUBLISHING

"What are some basic terms I should know as I get ready to self-publish? For instance, I know I will need to decide on a 'trim size' and provide 'cover matter.' I have no idea what this means."

I'm a big supporter of authors trying to self-publish their out-of-print works (and sometimes their new works, depending on the author and situation), and I've had a number of authors write to ask questions about publishing terms and traditions. I thought you might find it helpful to know some of the official nomenclature we use in the industry:

The TRIM SIZE is simply the size of the book. For instance, if you go to your local bookstore and pull a handful of trade paperbacks off the shelves, you will notice two of the most common sizes are 5.25 inches by 8 or 8.5 inches, or 6 inches by 9 inches. Mass market paperbacks (the spy or romance novels you usually see in Safeway and Wal-Mart) are a smaller trim size (about 4 or 4.25 by 6.5 or 6.75), and hard cover is generally 6 by 9, or larger, while the trade paperbacks *can* fall into various sizes in-between.

The FRONT MATTER is the information that goes in the front of the book, between the cover and the actual text. It usually contains a bunch of legal and technical information about the book, and the pages are numbered, though they usually aren't visible (at least not on what are called the "display" pages—the title page, the half title page, the copyright page, the dedication page, any blank pages, etc.).

There are a number of elements to the Front Matter that require special terms: the title page (which has the complete title, subtitle, author name, and publisher), the half-title page (which just has the book's title), the copyright page, the legal or copyright acknowledgements (if you needed permission for anything in your text), the dedication, acknowledgements, and table of contents. There may be a colophon, a more recent development in publishing a book that details the font, the printer, and any special production notes about the book.

There are also a number of additional Front Matter pieces used less often: a foreword (written by someone other than the author, to introduce the topic), perhaps a preface (written by the author to explain HOW the book was written), or an introduction (written by the author to explain WHY the book was written), a prologue (written by the narrator or a character in the novel to set the scene or give important background information), an epigraph (usually a poem or quote pertinent to the story), and the author's acknowledgements (so you can tell everyone how great your editor and agent have been in the process). The fact is, in recent days we've seen a decline in many of these. There's nothing more boring than picking up a book that has a foreword, a prologue, and introduction, and three pages of acknowledgments. By then, the reader has already fallen asleep.

The BODY MATTER is the text of the book—that is, the manuscript created by the author. These pages are numbered, and the numbers show on most every page. Special pages in between for chapter breaks, section breaks, book breaks, or part breaks (that is, a page that says "Part One," for example) normally don't have a visible number. Sometimes a publisher will make an artistic decision to leave the page numbers off of blank pages within the text or the first page of each chapter, but that's not the norm.

The BACK MATTER contains any content that is additional or subsidiary. Examples include footnotes, an index, a glossary, an appendix, or a bibliography. Occasionally, there will be an afterword (where the author says something about the creation of the book) or an epilogue (where the author brings closure to the story or explains what happened after the book was written). Other elements of Back Matter include an author bio and a list of other titles from the author. In recent years we've seen some of these elements move around—with author titles moved to the front, or acknowledgements moved to the back, but for the most part this is where the various pieces fit.

The COVER COPY is simply the text that will appear on your front cover—the title, subtitle (which may simply be the words "a novel"), and author name. Some nonfiction books will have additional information on the topic or the author to buttress the book's validity. Endorsements by celebrities or other well-known authors, in the form of a one line blurb supporting the book, are becoming popular but not commonplace. COVER MATTER is referring to the copy and the images that make up the front cover.

The BACK COVER COPY is everything that appears on the back cover. For most novels, that's a short elevator pitch to try and convince readers to get hooked on the story. For most nonfiction books, it's a selling tool to get the potential reader to crack open the book and look at the table of contents. It may or may not contain a brief author bio, or possibly an endorsement. Most publishers also lump the SPINE COPY in with back cover copy, and refer to it all as "BCC." Your spine will be limited to the title, author last name, and publisher imprimatur.

If you're releasing a hard cover book with a dust jacket, you will also have FRONT FLAP COPY and BACK FLAP COPY. The front flap of a novel offers a short synopsis for the story, and often replaces the back cover copy. The back flap of a hardcover novel will offer an author biography. With a nonfiction book, it's common for the summary to start on the front flap and continue to the back flap, before presenting a very brief author bio.

"How do you feel about ebooks?"

Any discussion of trends wouldn't be complete without mentioning the growth of ebooks and the shifting desires of readers to see books in other formats. I don't think ink-and-paper books are going away any time soon—most every reader still loves printed books. But I've got three kids in their 20s, and they are comfortable reading a book on a screen—even an iPhone screen. That tells me when their generation is in charge, the ebook will be the core business, not the side business. It has become a major part of every publishing decision, not simply a sub-rights discussion. Ebooks are . . . well, they're not the future. They are the present. They cost less to produce, so publishers actually make a greater percentage of profits on ebooks, which is helping keep traditional publishers in business.

The thing to understand is that we now have two universes of publishing—a traditional, heavily print-based universe, and a digital, ebook universe. When ebooks first released, they were seen as a different form of a printed book. Now they're seen as a completely different medium, just as audio books and films are different ways of sharing a story. So, while people in publishing took some time to fight over ebooks for a while (early adopters to ebooks saw traditional publishers as the enemy; and legacy publishers saw ebook authors as unedited purveyors of bad books), now we're seeing things shake out into these two worlds. And the upshot is that there are more opportunities than ever before. And, since I represent authors for a living, I see that as a good thing.

I'm the eternal optimist. We have more readers on this planet than ever before in the history of the world. We'll sell more books, in all the various forms, than ever before in the history of the world. What's not to like? Ebooks have been a boon for authors and publishers. I'm a huge fan.

"Are there companies that can help me format my manuscript so I can upload it as an ebook?"

Sure. There are a bunch. You can do it yourself by using Amazon's templates, or use the Smashwords formatting tools so it gets onto the iBookstore and B&N.com. There is a steep learning curve, though, so be prepared to spend time researching and practicing before you get it right, especially if you are trying to embed photos or illustrations. Formatting can be complicated if you aren't computer savvy, but there are plenty of manuals out there. Or you can skip the headache and go to a company like BookBaby (whom I've never used, but heard nice things about), which can do the basics for about two hundred bucks, but charge more if you need them to format before uploading the book. There are also smaller editorial and publishing services that will format a manuscript for ebook and POD, but be sure you trust their credentials if you find them on the internet, and do price comparisons; a benefit to going through a smaller company is the personal attention and service. Ebook assistance is a growing industry.

"Can you recommend a company that would be good for self-publishing a book of family photos and stories?"
You probably won't need more than fifty to seventy-five copies. The easy solution? Go to sites like Lulu.com or blurb.com or shutterfly.com, which make it easy to print small runs of books with a lot of photos, providing plenty of templates, design help, and customer service while you design and upload your project into the system. You will have to pay a fee for those services, but you've just saved yourself days, possibly weeks, of learning graphic design on a computer. You can go through CreateSpace at Amazon or the iBookstore, but you're on your own for design and uploading. And photos are particularly tricky. You end up paying more per book with the other sites, but that's the route I'd go if I were doing a small print run with a lot of pictures or text boxes.

"Which ebook publisher should I choose to print my novel?"
As I mentioned, I work with authors who are publishing with traditional publishers, as well as self-publishing some titles (known as hybrid authors). Several of them have asked: Which ebook publishers should I consider?

There are a number of choices for authors who want to indie-publish a book. Everybody tends to immediately think, "I'll just post it myself on Amazon," but we've seen countless error-filled books done on Amazon, so if you want to take a step forward, there are some options to consider. Of course, you need to know what you want in a publisher. For example, do you want to pay extra for marketing help? Does your nonfiction book need photos or maps in the text? Will you want the capability of adding an audio version of your novel? There are a bunch of choices, so let me suggest some places to consider checking out.

- Amazon's Kindle Direct Publishing (kdp.amazon.com). This is Amazon's ebook-only arm of their company, and can be a great choice for books with a simple design (image-heavy material is hard to manipulate) since it's quick and free. KDP will make sure your book is available on every Kindle and every computer or phone with the Kindle app (which is also free), it allows you to be part of their unlimited lending program, and has some special features such as their "countdown" deal and their free book program. KDP pays you a royalty of 35% of the list price on most sales, with the opportunity of a 70% royalty if you follow some pricing guidelines. They pay monthly, and can do direct deposits. It's a great way to go for many authors . . . but the big drawback is that they will have some Amazon-only restrictions. That means people who don't own a Kindle won't be seeing your book. Still, KDP is great for reaching the Kindle crowd, which is roughly 60% of all ebook readers.
- If you are looking to also publish Print On Demand paperbacks, then look into Amazon's free POD arm, called CreateSpace (www.createspace.com). You have to set up an account separate from your KDP account, but the sales information is merged in Amazon's catalog, so readers will find both options available when they search for your name or title. There are books available to help with formatting your manuscript, but you may need to pay a professional to format image-heavy pages. You will also probably need to hire a professional to create a print-ready cover.
- Smashwords (www.smashwords.com). This is who we almost always recommend to authors who want to reach beyond Amazon. Kindle is great, but Smashwords will get you into the iBookstore (for readers with iPads), the Nook bookstore (for Barnes & Noble devotees), the Kobo bookstore (which works with indie bookstores in this country, but is a big deal overseas), and Scribd. Instead of having to upload your titles to every

company independently, Smashwords takes care of all the non-Amazon e-tailers, and converts your text into the various formats you'll need. They also have nice extras such as free marketing help. They pay 70%, will send you checks quarterly, and we've never had a problem with the accounting at Smashwords. This is a company we trust, and if you self-publish through both Smashwords and Amazon, you're reaching all the major markets. I do suggest both, since Amazon has the lion's share of sales. And, like KDP and CreateSpace, you will need to format on your own, and supply a print-ready cover.

- BookBaby (www.bookbaby.com). This is a fast-growing company that makes it easy for authors. They offer three packages, charge you a flat fee, and can take care of everything—formatting, distributing to the e-tailers, and even helping with marketing. They have some great extra features (like an author bookstore page, or good cover design assistance) that cost more, but the authors I've spoken with have been very happy with their experiences at BookBaby. This is more of a one-stop shopping—so while posting your POD book on Amazon is free, the convenience of using BookBaby will cost you, but it might be worth it. They pay 85% of net. BookBaby isn't as fast as the others, but they have good customer service, and offer some really nice extra features (that you'll have to pay for, of course). We think they're a good option for the right authors.

- Kobo's Writing Life (www.kobo.com). This one might be new to you, but I mention it because it's huge in other countries. Kobo currently says they are the world's second-largest ebookstore, and that they're doing book in nearly seventy languages, reaching into almost two hundred countries (that's from their website, so I'm taking their word for it). I've known authors who have worked with them, and they rave about how easy it is—you upload a file, Kobo converts it, they pay you 70%, and they're now starting to offer some marketing helps. But the big news is that they're working closely with ABA bookstores, which means all those indie bookstores will be helping you to sell your titles. This is one of those companies you might be overlooking, so make sure to check them out.

There are certainly others. Apple has iBook Author, (which people have complained is cumbersome to use, but can be great for children's books, cookbooks, or projects with photos), NookPress (which replaced PubIt, is easy to use, but only for those who own the floundering Nook), Vook (which can work with all the e-tailers, but works on a different economic model than the others), eBookIt (the competitor to BookBaby in terms of being a one-stop shop), and BookTango, iUniverse, Trafford, and Lulu, who are all owned or in partnership with the folks at AuthorSolutions. To anyone looking at an AuthorSolutions company, I always say, "Do your research." There are good programs and bad programs, but understand that AuthorSolutions is too often accused of being there to sell services to you, as the author, not to necessarily sell books to consumers.

"I was sent an ebook contract from a small publisher, and it demands all rights, forever, plus POD rights. Are there things I should look for in an ebook contract?"

There are a bunch of things to look for in any publishing contract, including: What rights are you granting them? Is this just U.S. or also foreign rights? Do they want dramatic rights? When is the manuscript due? What are the royalty rates? What is the royalty based on? How often am I paid? Is there a reserve clause? When will they publish it? What's the process if they don't like my manuscript? What does the competing works clause look like? What is the duration of this contract? How do rights get reverted to me?

What you're describing sounds like a rights-grab from an unscrupulous publisher. My advice: If you don't know contracts, talk to someone who does. A contract is a legally binding document that will govern the entire business side of your book for as long as it's in print. That being the case, you owe it to yourself to get it right. You probably wouldn't buy a house without having someone knowledgeable help you with the contract—treat your books the same way.

"If I indie publish some of my books, will an agent represent me at traditional houses with other titles?"

Usually, yes, agents will work with writers to place some of their titles at houses while the author has retained the rights to other titles and he or she is selling those books independently. This type of author is called a *hybrid author*. In today's market, this trending career strategy makes a lot of sense, especially if the author can quickly produce books.

"How can I become a hybrid author?"

I'm frequently asked about the notion of working with hybrid authors because I seem to be a bit in the minority—a literary agent who actually *encourages* his authors to become hybrids. But you see, I used to make my living as a writer, so I understand what it's like to try and make a living creating words. And the changes in the industry that have taken place means there are new opportunities available to writers that were never available in the past.

As I said, a hybrid author is one who is self-publishing *and* traditionally publishing. There are plenty of people who insist one method or the other is the "right" way to have a writing career these days—that you either "get an advance and publish your books with a legacy press and ignore the badly-edited self-published crud on Amazon," *or* you "self-publish your title via Amazon and Smashwords, and reject those money-grubbing publishers in New York who only want to enslave you as a midlist author." Um . . . I tend to think there's another way.

A hybrid author gets the benefit of an occasional advance check, professional editing, great distribution, and access to marketing professionals from his or her publisher. Plus there's the benefit of having complete creative control, book price control, and the chance to do more titles that generate immediate earnings from his or her self-published titles.

Of course, there's also a downside. A hybrid author really has to set up his or her writing life as a small business, since everything from cover choices to copyediting payments are the responsibility of the author. He or she has to stay up on trends—which e-tailers are selling your books? What formats are selling best? What price points? What changes do you have to make to stay current? How do I line up my self-published books with my traditional releases? And for most hybrid authors, marketing becomes a full-time job. With that sort of to-do list, simply finding time to write can be difficult.

So, the decision to become a hybrid author is really the decision to start your own company—one where you'll be making the decisions, handling the problems, and charting your own strategic direction.

Each author is different, so your needs won't be the same as someone else's, but some writers really need help with editing, others with managing the business, still others with handling all the marketing responsibilities. A good agent ought to be able to help an author manage relationships, coordinate with publishers, and troubleshoot the difficult issues you face. He or she may be able to help with vendor coordination or marketing planning. Most importantly, an agent really ought to be able to help you clarify your long-term goals and create a plan for reaching them.

But authors aren't limited to simply publishing with a huge New York house or self-publishing their manuscript on their own. The changes in technology and the advent of ebooks has created a brand new world of indie publishers—smaller houses who are sometimes doing e-only titles, and sometimes doing ebook and print-on-demand books, often marketing them to a niche audience. This has greatly expanded the options available to authors, as companies step in to assist authors with reaching their readers.

If you're a writer pondering what steps to take to become a hybrid author, let me suggest a few simple things to consider. First, look at the books you already have scheduled, and the manuscripts you've completed and want to self-publish. Begin to map out a schedule of releases that gets you out there on the market, but doesn't have you competing with yourself. You're going to do best as a hybrid author if you have several titles to sell to the same readership, or you can keep creating new works, and you decide to sell them at a price the market will support. Start by creating a publishing plan for your titles.

Second, begin to create a list of people in your world who can help you move forward—editors, marketing professionals, cover designers, and people with the technical experience to assist you in the process. You may need to be talking to someone who can help with foreign rights, or with someone who can help with dramatic rights. You may need to sit down with a business manager or accountant to assist with the financial picture.

Third, determine right now that you're going to invest a lot of time into marketing. That's the most important skill you're going to need if you plan to set up a self-publishing business, so that could mean investing in some training or resources, or deciding to link up with some experienced marketing types who can assist you in this new venture. Most authors get into hybrid publishing having done some publicity, but with little experience mapping out a marketing plan, and almost none with advertising. So, boning up on those areas by taking classes or talking with experts in the field can help you move forward.

One author I represent, Vincent Zandri, decided several years ago he was going to become a hybrid author. He has worked with traditional publishers, and currently has created a handful of bestselling books with Thomas & Mercer, a publishing house imprint at Amazon. But he has also worked with smaller houses, *and* has successfully self-published some titles, so that he has maximum exposure to readers. The result? Over the past four years, Vince has sold hundreds of thousands of books, landed on the New York Times bestseller list, and made a good living as a writer.

Hybrid publishing isn't for everyone, but it might be an avenue to consider if you're an entrepreneurial and prolific writer with a knack for marketing.

"What's the best way to market my ebook so that it stands out on Amazon?"

That's the million-dollar question, isn't it? There is no easy or even straightforward answer I can give you. If you have chosen to self-publish, please understand that marketing has now become a permanent job for you, or you will need to hire a publicist, at least if you want to sell copies. There's no one-time silver bullet, either. You'll have to do book tours, book blogs, media interviews, go to bookstores to ask them to put your book on the shelf . . . and so much more.

The best place to get started is to find yourself a couple of good reference books in regards to marketing ebooks. If what you are really trying to do is to game Amazon's sales algorithms, good luck. Again, be wary of anyone who is offering you instant success on Amazon, or is guaranteeing they can get you on a bestselling list, they are either crazy or scam artists. I do have a list of trustworthy books referenced on my blog, including *The Extroverted Writer: An Author's Guide to Marketing and Building a Platform* by MacGregor Literary's own Amanda Luedeke.

I'm really not trying to be coy here, purposefully withholding information just so you'll buy another book; this is a question you will have to take some time to research, and then make your own decisions regarding how much time you want to spend and what you are willing to do to sell your book.

Best of wishes on your publishing journey.

ACKNOWLEDGEMENTS

My thanks to Holly, Amanda, Marie, Erin, Sandra, Shannon, Hannah, Buzz, Karen, Brian, and all the people who have worked with me at MacGregor Literary over the years, for helping me be successful at this gig. Additional thanks go to the folks at The Writers View (who first got me answering questions), those at Novel Journey, and the people running ACFW, Blue Ridge, RWA, and numerous other conferences who gave me a chance to figure out what the questions were, and what needed to be said. Thanks also to Steve, Janet, Wendy, Greg, Natasha, and my other agent friends, for offering wisdom on questions I didn't know anything about, and to all those who came to my blog to ask great questions. Finally, thanks to Keri Knudsen at Alchemy Covers for creating the cover, Heidi Gray and Erin Buterbaugh for reviewing the text, and Holly Lorincz for putting all of this together.
—*Chip MacGregor*

Made in the USA
Charleston, SC
23 December 2015